THE COMPREHENSIVE DUMMIES GUIDE TO STARTING YOUR OWN BUSINESS

REID ROADMAP

1

CONTENTS

COPYRIGHT 1

CONTENTS 2

PART 1: INTRODUCTION TO ENTREPRENEURSHIP 4

  1 THE ENTREPRENEURIAL JOURNEY 4

  2 SELF-ASSESSMENT 8

PART 2: FINDING YOUR BUSINESS IDEA. 14

  3 IDEA GENERATION 14

  4 MARKET RESEARCH 23

PART 3: PLANNING YOUR BUSINESS. 32

  5 BUSINESS PLANNING BASICS 32

  6 FINANCIAL PLANNING 38

PART 4: LEGAL AND FINANCIAL CONSIDERATIONS. 45

  7 CHOOSING A LEGAL STRUCTURE 45

  8 FUNDING YOUR BUSINESS 52

PART 5: SETTING UP YOUR BUSINESS. 59

  9 REGISTERING YOUR BUSINESS 59

  10 LOCATION AND WORKSPACE 66

PART 6: MARKETING AND SALES. 73

  11 MARKETING STRATEGIES 73

  CHAPTER 12 SALES AND CUSTOMER ACQUISITION .. 81

PART 7: OPERATIONS AND MANAGEMENT. 88

  13 OPERATIONS AND PROCESSES 88

  14 TEAM BUILDING AND MANAGEMENT 94

PART 8: SCALING AND GROWTH... 100

   15 SCALING YOUR BUSINESS 100

   16 MANAGING FINANCES FOR GROWTH 106

PART 9: TROUBLESHOOTING AND CHALLENGES. 112

   17 TROUBLESHOOTING AND CHALLENGES............... 112

   18 EXIT STRATEGIES 118

CONCLUSION... 121

1

THE ENTREPRENEURIAL JOURNEY

Entrepreneurship: A Simple Definition

Entrepreneurship, in its simplest form, is about turning ideas into successful enterprises. It's the art of discovering opportunities, solving issues, and generating value for others in a manner that maintains itself and ideally, expands over time. At the basis of entrepreneurship is the desire to take measured risks and to undertake the responsibility of establishing something from the beginning.

The Essence of Entrepreneurship

Entrepreneurship isn't only about startups and tech enterprises. It's an attitude, a method of thinking and doing that can be applied to any business, at every stage of life. You don't need to be a Silicon Valley visionary to be an entrepreneur. In truth, entrepreneurship may be as much about tiny enterprises, family-owned firms, and freelancing as it is about billion-dollar unicorns.

Entrepreneurs perceive possibilities where others would see hurdles. They are motivated by their vision and their passion, and they possess a unique capacity to take an idea and transform it into a reality. They're problem solvers, and inventors, and frequently, they're disruptors.

4

Starting a Business as an Entrepreneur

If you're thinking about establishing a company, you're already on the road to entrepreneurship. Whether you've had a lifetime ambition of running a local coffee shop, or you've stumbled onto a new invention, the first step is embracing your entrepreneurial spirit.

Entrepreneurship is a journey with several stages. It starts with ideation, the act of developing and accessing company ideas. Then comes the planning step, when you put your concept into a defined company strategy. You'll register your firm, acquire money, and choose a site. Once operational, you'll transfer your emphasis to marketing, sales, operations, and management. Finally, you'll examine expansion and growth, or possibly even departure alternatives.

The beauty of entrepreneurship is that it's not a one-size-fits-all path. Your journey will be unique, molded by your vision and the particular problems and opportunities you meet. It's a voyage defined by uncertainty, but also by the potential for enormous rewards.

In essence, entrepreneurship is the quest for freedom, the desire to build something of your own, and the idea that you can make a difference in the world. So, let's go on this entrepreneurial adventure together and discover the ins and outs of founding and maintaining a successful firm. We'll learn how to handle the hurdles, grasp the chances, and transform your idea become a reality.

What to Expect as an ENTREPRENEUR?

Embarking on the entrepreneurial road is an exhilarating and, at times, hard effort. While each entrepreneur's route is unique, there are similar components and experiences that you can anticipate along the road. In this chapter, we'll cover what you should expect when you embark into the realm of business.

1. Uncertainty and Risk:

Entrepreneurship is fundamentally unpredictable. You'll confront concerns such as, "Will my business succeed?" and "What if it fails?" These uncertainties might be disconcerting, but they're a vital part of the trip. Expect to make judgments with inadequate knowledge and learn to handle risks efficiently.

2. Passion and Dedication:

As an entrepreneur, your love for your concept or firm is a driving force. You'll put in hard hours and experience setbacks, but your devotion will keep you going. Expect to be fueled by your passion and the feeling that what you're doing matters.

3. Learning and Adaptation:

Be prepared to always learn and adjust. You'll need to gain new abilities, remain current on industry trends, and alter your strategy as circumstances change. Expect a high learning curve, and consider every problem as a chance for progress.

4. Financial Fluctuations:

Your financial status may be uncertain, particularly in the early phases. There will be moments when you invest your own money, get finance, or depend on income. Expect financial ups and downs, and handle your resources prudently.

5. Work-Life Balance:

Entrepreneurship may be hard, and maintaining a work-life balance can be a problem. Expect to juggle various obligations, but also endeavor to establish balance. Your well-being is vital for your business's success.

6. Independence and Decision-Making:

One of the delights of business is the freedom it affords. You'll have the flexibility to make choices, determine your path, and create the firm according to your vision. Expect to embrace this liberty but also accept responsibility for your decisions.

7. Resilience and Perseverance:

Challenges are unavoidable, and setbacks are part of the business path. Expect to confront misfortune, but also build resilience. You'll learn to bounce back from failures and keep going ahead.

8. Network and Relationships:

Entrepreneurship is a social effort. You'll connect with mentors, advisers, other entrepreneurs, consumers, and possible partners. Expect to create a beneficial network of contacts that may give assistance and opportunities.

9. Innovation and Creativity:

Entrepreneurs are inventors. You'll need to think creatively, solve difficulties, and come up with fresh ideas to distinguish your firm. Expect to embrace innovation as a vital aspect of your job.

10. Impact and Fulfillment:

Ultimately, entrepreneurship is about creating a real difference. You have the potential to develop goods or services that enhance people's lives. Expect to find satisfaction in the impact you make in your career and your community.

As you begin on your entrepreneurial journey, remember that it's not only about reaching a goal; it's about the experiences, development, and learning that occur along the way. Embrace the obstacles and appreciate the benefits that come with business. In the chapters to follow, we'll go further into each element and give directions to help you navigate the entrepreneurial route effectively.

2

SELF-ASSESSMENT

Identifying Your Strengths and Weaknesses

Before you delve deeply into business, it's vital to take a step back and analyze yourself honestly. Understanding your talents and shortcomings is the basis upon which you may construct a successful company. In this chapter, we'll cover the process of self-assessment and how to determine what you offer to the entrepreneurial table.

Recognizing Your Strengths

Your strengths are your distinct benefits as an entrepreneur. They are the characteristics, abilities, and attributes that will move you ahead and set you distinct. Here's how to identify your strengths:

1. Self-Reflection: Take some time for reflection. What are you actually enthusiastic about? What activities invigorate you? Your interests frequently correlate with your talents.

2. Skill Inventory: Assess your skills. What are you extremely excellent at? This might be anything from problem-solving and leadership to technical skills or creativity.

3. Feedback from Others: Sometimes, your friends, family, or coworkers may give helpful insights about your talents. They may have spotted features in you that you take for granted.

4. prior Successes: Reflect on your prior triumphs, no matter how minor they may appear. What led to your successes? This might expose your strengths in action.

5. Personality characteristics: Your personality characteristics might be strengths. Are you naturally extroverted and persuasive? Are you detail-oriented and organized? These traits might be advantages in various entrepreneurial professions.

6. Values and Beliefs: Consider your essential values and beliefs. What ideals govern your decisions? These principles may be a source of strength, giving a solid foundation for your firm.

Acknowledging Your Weaknesses

Identifying your limitations is just as vital as acknowledging your strengths. Knowing where you could need help or improvement might avert possible mistakes. Here's how to admit your weaknesses:

1. Feedback and Assessment: Seek feedback from others, particularly those who are honest with you. What areas do they believe you might improve upon?

2. Self-Reflection: Be open with yourself. Are there duties or obligations that you prefer to avoid or struggle with? These places could expose your inadequacies.

3. Skill Gaps: Identify areas where you lack certain abilities or expertise. These gaps might represent potential vulnerabilities.

4. prior Failures: Reflect on prior failures or struggles. What contributed to such failures? Understanding the shortcomings that played a role will help you fix them.

5. Overextension: Are you attempting to accomplish too much on your own? Sometimes, overextending oneself might show your limits.

6. Personality qualities: Certain personality qualities, although assets in certain contexts, may become drawbacks in others. For example, perfectionism may lead to procrastination.

Leveraging Your Findings

Once you've discovered your skills and limitations, it's important to exploit this information. Here's how:

1. Build on talents: Focus on exploiting your talents to drive your company. Delegate responsibilities that coincide with your shortcomings to individuals who thrive in those areas.

2. Skill Development: Invest in self-improvement. If you've found skill gaps, try training, classes, or mentoring to reinforce your shortcomings.

3. Collaboration: Seek partners or team members who complement your abilities and shortcomings. A well-rounded workforce can cover all parts of the company successfully.

4. Outsourcing: For activities that aren't in your wheelhouse, consider outsourcing to specialists or service providers. This might free up your time to concentrate on what you do best.

5. Continuous Self-Assessment: Self-assessment isn't a one-time practice. Regularly evaluate your strengths and shortcomings as your firm changes and you grow as an entrepreneur.

By evaluating your skills and limitations, you'll be better prepared to make educated choices and establish a company that plays to your strengths while limiting the effect of your flaws. In the chapters that follow, we'll dig into how to apply this self-awareness to the numerous areas of entrepreneurship, from company planning to team development and beyond.

Assessing Your Readiness for Entrepreneurship

Before taking the jump into business, it's vital to evaluate your preparation for this tough and rewarding path. Starting a company involves not just self-awareness but also a realistic appraisal of your existing circumstances and your desire to change. In this chapter, we'll study ways to measure your preparation for entrepreneurship.

Evaluating Your Commitment

Entrepreneurship takes a serious commitment. You'll commit time, energy, and resources to your firm, typically with unclear returns in the beginning stages. Here's how to judge your commitment:

1. Passion and Purpose: Are you enthusiastic about your company idea? Entrepreneurship is a long-term undertaking, and your enthusiasm will propel you through tough times.

2. Risk Tolerance: Consider your risk tolerance. Are you okay with the unpredictability and financial risk involved with entrepreneurship? Can you handle stress effectively?

3. Time Allocation: Assess your present obligations and duties. Are you willing to commit a large percentage of your time to your business? Entrepreneurship may be difficult, especially in the early years.

4. Financial Preparedness: Review your financial status. Do you have savings or access to cash to help your firm through its earliest phases? How will you handle your own funds during this period?

Skills and Knowledge

Entrepreneurship demands a varied range of skills and expertise. Assess your present talents and identify areas where you may need to progress or seek support:

1. Industry Knowledge: Do you have a thorough grasp of the industry in which you want to launch your business? If not, are you eager to study and investigate extensively?

2. Business Acumen: How well do you comprehend the key concepts of operating a business? If you lack this information, are you open to gaining it via classes, seminars, or mentorship?

3. Networking Skills: Building and maintaining a network of relationships is vital in business. Do you have good networking abilities, or do you need to concentrate on growing your professional relationships?

4. Problem-Solving and Decision-Making: Assess your abilities to solve issues and make choices under pressure. These talents are crucial in the entrepreneurial environment.

Personal Attributes

Entrepreneurship typically requires unique personal traits. Reflect on your talents and how they connect with the demands of entrepreneurship:

1. Resilience: Can you bounce back from losses and remain motivated in the face of adversity?

2. Self-motivation: Entrepreneurship frequently includes self-direction. Are you self-motivated and disciplined?

3. Adaptability: Evaluate your adaptability. Are you open to change and comfortable with ambiguity?

4. Leadership and Communication: Effective leadership and communication abilities are crucial. How do you evaluate your ability in these areas?

Support System

Entrepreneurship doesn't have to be a solo endeavor. Assess the support system available to you:

1. Family and Friends: What is the degree of assistance you may anticipate from your family and friends? Will they comprehend the time and energy you need to devote to your business?

2. Mentors and advisers: Do you have access to experienced mentors or advisers who can give assistance and insights?

3. Financial Safety Net: Consider if you have a financial safety net, such as savings or part-time work, to give stability throughout the early phases of your firm.

4. Business Network: Assess your present business network. Are there possible partners, collaborators, or customers among your contacts?

Vision and Goals

Lastly, think about your vision for your company and your long-term goals:

1. Business Vision: Clearly outline your business vision. What do you aim to accomplish, and what influence do you want to make?

2. Long-Term Objectives: Consider your long-term objectives. Are you prepared for the commitment necessary to attain them?

3. departure plan: Even from the beginning, think about your prospective departure plan. Do you anticipate yourself operating the company for the long term, or do you have plans for selling or transitioning out?

By completing a comprehensive self-assessment and evaluating these characteristics, you may acquire a better image of your preparedness for entrepreneurship. Remember that preparedness isn't fixed; it's something you can grow and build as you advance on your business path. In the ensuing chapters, we'll dig into the practical procedures and methods to prepare yourself for entrepreneurship and take you through the process of beginning and operating your firm.

3

IDEA GENERATION

Techniques for Brainstorming Business Ideas

Every successful company begins with a fantastic concept. Whether you have a clear concept in mind or you're beginning from scratch, the process of brainstorming company ideas is both creative and strategic. In this chapter, we'll discuss ways to help you produce and enhance your company ideas.

1. Problem-Solution Approach

One of the most successful methods to create company ideas is by finding issues or unmet requirements in the market and generating solutions for them. Here's how to implement this approach:

• Market study: Conduct a detailed study to identify the pain areas, problems, or gaps in the market.

• Customer Interviews: Talk to prospective customers to acquire insights into their challenges and wants.

• Brainstorm Solutions: Generate a list of prospective solutions, goods, or services that solve the highlighted challenges.

2. SWOT Analysis

A SWOT analysis (Strengths, Weaknesses, Opportunities, and Threats) is a systematic way to evaluate company concepts. Here's how to utilize it for idea generation:

• qualities: List your own qualities, talents, and resources. How can you harness them to generate a business idea?

• Weaknesses: Recognize areas where you could require help or development.

• possibilities: Identify rising trends, market possibilities, or untapped areas.

• Threats: Consider possible hurdles, rivals, and problems you may encounter.

3. Mind Mapping

Mind mapping is a creative technique to examine numerous facets of a company concept. Start with a key notion and construct a visual map of related concepts, relationships, and possibilities.

• Central concept: Write your fundamental company concept in the middle of a blank page.

• Branches: Create branches that reflect distinct components of the concept, such as target market, income sources, and value propositions.

• Expand: Expand each branch with more comprehensive sub-ideas and linkages.

4. Reverse Engineering

Start with an existing successful company or product and work backward to uncover changes or enhancements you may make. Here's how to implement this technique:

• Select a Model: Choose a successful company or product you respect or find fascinating.

• Deconstruction: Analyze its essential components, such as its company strategy, client base, and marketing methods.

• Innovation: Brainstorm methods to innovate, distinguish, or improve upon the current model to establish your distinct company concept.

5. Problem Diary

Keep a "problem diary" where you write down issues you experience in your everyday life or notice in the lives of others. Over time, check your notes to uncover reoccurring difficulties that might be the foundation for a company concept.

• Daily Observations: Record difficulties or inconveniences you face, regardless matter how little they may appear.

• Patterns and Trends: Look for patterns or trends among the issues you've identified.

• Idea Development: For recurrent or severe concerns, explore ideas or services that might solve them.

6. Ideation Workshops

Collaborative brainstorming sessions also referred to as ideation workshops, involve a group of individuals working together to produce ideas. Here's how to conduct one:

• Diverse Participants: Invite persons with varied experiences, talents, and viewpoints to guarantee a broad variety of ideas.

• Creative activities: Use creativity-enhancing activities, such as word association, mind mapping, and role-play situations.

• Open Dialogue: Encourage open and non-judgmental talks to develop innovative thinking.

7. Hobbies and Passions

Consider your hobbies, interests, and passions as possible sources of company ideas. Think about how your own passions may be converted into commercial companies.

• Hobby Exploration: Reflect on your hobbies and interests. What components of your interests may be monetized?

• Market Demand: Research whether there's a demand in the market for items or services linked to your hobbies.

• Alignment: Look for possibilities where your own interests meet with market demands.

8. Competitor Analysis

Analyze current firms within your selected sector or specialty. Identify gaps or places where competitors may not be completely addressing client needs:

• Market Gaps: Investigate what your rivals are providing and where they may fall short.

• consumer Feedback: Read reviews and collect consumer feedback to highlight areas for improvement.

• Innovation: Brainstorm methods to develop improved goods or services to solve the identified gaps.

9. Trend Watching

Keep an eye on upcoming trends and technology. Identifying the next big thing or capitalizing on a burgeoning trend might lead to unique company ideas.

• Industry Trends: Research trends and developments within your industry or similar industries.

• Consumer Behavior: Understand how developing consumer behavior affects market needs.

• Technology Advancements: Consider how new technology may be leveraged to generate unique solutions.

10. Feedback from Others

Don't underestimate the significance of obtaining input from friends, family, coworkers, or future consumers. They may give ideas and viewpoints that you hadn't considered.

• Idea Pitch: Share your company proposal with others and seek for their comments.

• Critical Questions: Encourage them to ask questions and criticize your notion, which may lead to useful changes.

• varied Input: Gather comments from a varied set of individuals to gain a well-rounded viewpoint.

Remember that idea creation is an iterative process. It may take time to improve your early ideas into a successful company plan. Be open to integrating numerous ideas and strategies to produce a company concept that not only excites you but also connects with your target audience. In the chapters ahead, we'll examine ways to validate and develop your company ideas further.

Identifying Market Opportunities

Once you've developed a variety of company ideas, the next critical step is to discover market possibilities. A market opportunity is a gap or unmet need in the market that your organization can fill. In this part, we'll study how to discover and assess these prospects.

1. Market Research

Comprehensive market research is the cornerstone of discovering market opportunities. Here's how to perform excellent research:

• Target Audience Analysis: Understand your prospective consumers. What are their preferences, pain spots, and needs?

• Competitive Landscape: Analyze your competition. What items or services are already on the market? How do they satisfy or fail to meet client demands?

• Market Trends: Stay current on industry trends and market movements. What fresh developments or movements might offer chances for your business?

• Customer Surveys: Directly connect with prospective consumers via surveys and interviews to obtain useful data.

2. Problem Validation

Once you've discovered an issue or need, it's vital to confirm it. Ensure that the problem you've found is actually important and that people are prepared to pay for a solution.

• Customer Feedback: Seek feedback from your target audience via surveys, focus groups, or one-on-one interactions.

• Pilot Testing: Consider performing small-scale pilot testing or delivering a minimum viable product (MVP) to assess the market's reaction.

• Prototyping: If applicable, produce prototypes or sample items to illustrate your solution to prospective buyers.

3. Gap Analysis

Perform a gap analysis to discover areas where the market is underserved or where current solutions fall short.

• Market Gaps: What particular gaps or weaknesses exist in the present offerings in your industry?

• Customer Pain Points: Identify the pain points or issues that consumers have in your selected market.

• Unexplored Niches: Look for niches or sub-markets within your sector that have been ignored or underserved.

4. Market Size and Growth Potential

Assess the size and growth potential of the market opportunity. A bigger market with strong growth potential might be more enticing to investors and give opportunities for your organization to develop.

• Market Size: Determine the total addressable market (TAM) to comprehend the size of the client base.

• Market Growth: Investigate if the market is increasing, steady, or shrinking. An expanding market gives additional chances.

5. Competitive Analysis

Understand your rivals and the competitive environment within the defined market opportunity.

• Competitor Strengths and Weaknesses: Analyze your rivals' strengths and weaknesses to uncover areas where you can exceed them.

• distinctive Selling Proposition (USP): Determine what distinctive value your firm may give that sets you apart from the competition.

6. Regulatory and Legal Considerations

Research the legal and regulatory environment relevant to your company concept. Understanding the legal limits and regulations might help you discover possible possibilities and obstacles.

• Licensing and Compliance: Determine whether your company concept needs certain licenses or compliances and the related procedures.

• Intellectual Property: Investigate if you need to protect your intellectual property via patents, trademarks, or copyrights.

7. Emerging Technologies and Trends

Stay updated about developing technology and trends that might influence your industry. These advances may generate new possibilities for inventive firms.

• Technology Integration: Explore how cutting-edge technology, such as artificial intelligence or blockchain, may be implemented into your organization.

• Changing customer Behavior: Observe changes in customer behavior, such as a preference for eco-friendly items or online purchasing.

8. Networking and Partnerships

Build a network of connections in your sector to uncover chances for cooperation and collaboration.

• Industry Events: Attend industry conferences, trade exhibitions, and networking events to meet with possible partners.

• Alliances: Explore collaborations with other firms, suppliers, or organizations that may help your company expand.

9. Geographic Expansion

Consider if there are prospects to develop your firm regionally. Sometimes, a successful company model in one place may be copied in other locations.

• Market Saturation: Assess if your firm has reached a point of market saturation in its present location.

• Market Research: Research prospective new sites and do market research to understand local tastes and requirements.

10. Environmental and Social Responsibility

Increasingly, people are searching for firms that exhibit social and environmental responsibility. Identify chances to integrate sustainability and social impact into your company.

• friendly Practices: Explore strategies to make your company operations more ecologically friendly.

• Social Initiatives: Consider how your firm may contribute to social causes or help local communities.

By carefully assessing these elements, you may find particular market possibilities that correspond with your company concept and your aspirations as an entrepreneur. It's crucial to remember that market prospects may alter, therefore continual research and adaptability are key to remaining relevant and successful in the dynamic world of business. In future chapters, we'll go into how to verify your company idea and construct a sound business strategy based on your discovered market prospects

4

MARKET RESEARCH

Conducting Market Research to Validate Your Idea

Market research is a crucial stage in the road of converting your company concept into a profitable operation. It helps you acquire critical data, obtain insights into your target audience, and establish if there's a need for your product or service. In this chapter, we'll go into the process of performing market research to verify your proposal.

1. Define Your Research Objectives

Before you go into the research process, it's necessary to explicitly establish your study objectives. What particular questions or components of your company concept do you wish to validate? For example:

• Is there a need for my product or service?

• Who is my target audience, and what are their preferences?

• Who are my competitors, and what are their strengths and weaknesses?

• What is the cost range for comparable goods or services in the market?

Having a specific grasp of what you need to confirm can lead your research efforts efficiently.

2. Identify Your Target Audience

Understanding your target audience is a vital part of market research. Your audience's tastes, demands, and habits will affect all elements of your organization, from product creation to marketing. Here's how to identify and analyze your target audience:

• Demographics: Define the age, gender, geography, economic level, and other demographic aspects of your prospective clients.

• Psychographics: Explore their lifestyle, values, interests, and purchase behaviors.

• Market Segmentation: Divide your target into categories based on common features to adapt your approach.

• Surveys and Interviews: Conduct surveys or interviews with persons who suit your target audience to obtain information straight from them.

3. Competitive Analysis

Analyzing your competition is a crucial component of validating your company concept. It helps you comprehend the competition environment, find gaps in the market, and enhance your unique selling offer. Here's how to perform competitive analysis:

• List Competitors: Compile a list of firms or items that compete with your concept.

• Strengths and Weaknesses: Assess their strengths and weaknesses in terms of product quality, marketing methods, price, and customer service.

• Differentiation: Identify how your firm may stand out from the competition and provide something distinctive.

• Competitor Pricing: Study the pricing methods of your rivals to help define your price range.

4. Surveys and Questionnaires

Surveys and questionnaires are great tools for obtaining data and feedback from your target audience. They may help you measure interest in your proposal and find possible obstacles. Here's how to utilize polls effectively:

• Design Clear Questions: Craft brief and clear questions that connect to your study goals.

• Select a Survey Tool: Choose an online survey tool or conduct in-person surveys.

• Sample Size: Ensure your sample size is statistically significant to deliver reliable findings.

• Analyze Data: Analyze the acquired data to make relevant conclusions.

5. Interviews

One-on-one interviews help you to dive further into the thoughts and opinions of prospective consumers. They give a more in-depth grasp of your target audience's wants and preferences. Consider the following:

• Open-Ended Questions: Use open-ended questions to encourage participants to share their ideas and experiences.

• varied Participants: Interview a varied range of individuals within your target audience to get a wide spectrum of viewpoints.

• Active Listening: Be an active listener and dig further to acquire a better grasp of the replies.

6. Observational Research

Observational research entails actually viewing your target audience in their natural habitat. This might be especially effective for goods or services that entail certain customer habits.

• Field Research: Observe how prospective clients engage with items or services comparable to your proposal.

• Note-Taking: Take extensive notes during observations to capture trends and behaviors.

• Ethnographic Studies: Consider ethnographic studies, where researchers immerse themselves in the everyday lives of individuals.

7. Online Presence and Social Media

Your prospective clients regularly communicate their demands and preferences online. Monitor social media platforms, internet forums, and review sites to obtain insights:

• Social Listening: Use social listening tools to monitor mentions, debates, and feelings linked to your concept.

• Feedback Analysis: Analyze comments and reviews to determine what customers like or find missing in comparable goods or services.

8. Secondary Research

Secondary research entails leveraging existing sources of data and information to inform your market research. It can save time and costs by using current research:

• Industry publications: Access industry-specific publications and market studies that give insights into trends and consumer habits.

• Government Data: Explore data produced by government agencies or organizations that may apply to your market.

• scholarly Research: Review scholarly papers that address themes related to your company concept.

9. Prototype Testing

If appropriate, construct a prototype or minimum viable product (MVP) to test with your target audience. Their input may confirm whether your product or service fits their demands.

• Solicit comments: Encourage users to offer comments on the usability, functionality, and overall experience of the prototype.

• Iterate and Improve: Use the input to enhance your prototype and iterate until it matches market expectations.

10. Analyze and Synthesize Data

Once you've obtained data from numerous sources, the following step is to evaluate and synthesize it. Look for patterns, ideas, and trends that verify or challenge your company concept. Ensure that your analysis matches your primary study aims.

11. Adjust Your Idea

Market research is not only about verifying your original concept; it's also a chance to change and develop it depending on the insights you've acquired. Be flexible in adjusting your company idea to better fit the demands and preferences of your target audience.

By completing extensive market research, you'll be better positioned to verify your company concept and make educated judgments as you go ahead. The information you receive will also be beneficial when you start constructing your company strategy. In the next chapters, we'll cover the processes to improve your concept and establish a strong strategy for your firm.

Understanding Your Target Audience

To effectively validate and develop your company concept, it's vital to obtain a comprehensive knowledge of your target customer. Your audience's tastes, demands, and behaviors will drive your company strategy, from product design to marketing. In this chapter, we'll discuss how to completely know your target audience.

1. Define Your Ideal Customer

Start by building a clear and thorough description of your ideal client or buyer persona. Your buyer persona should comprise crucial features, including:

• Demographics: Age, gender, location, income level, education, and employment.

• Psychographics: Lifestyle, values, interests, hobbies, and attitudes.

• Behavioral Traits: Buying patterns, brand preferences, and online activity.

• obstacles and Pain Points: Identify the difficulties or obstacles people encounter that your firm can answer.

2. Conduct Surveys and Questionnaires

Surveys and questionnaires are great tools for getting information from your prospective clients. Craft well-structured surveys with clear and simple questions that connect to your research goals. Ensure that you capture data on:

• Product Preferences: Understand what sorts of items or services they presently use or are interested in.

• Pain Points: Identify their issues, needs, and pain points that your firm can help with.

• Communication Preferences: Learn about their favorite communication methods and how they absorb information.

• Feedback and recommendations: Encourage responders to contribute feedback and recommendations about your company concept.

3. Interviews and Focus Groups

One-on-one interviews and focus groups enable you to delve deeper into the thoughts and opinions of your prospective clients. When conducting interviews and focus groups:

• Open-Ended Questions: Use open-ended questions to encourage people to share their experiences and stories.

• issues and ambitions: Probe deeper to learn the issues they confront and their ambitions and aspirations.

• impressions of Competitors: Ask about their impressions of current goods or services in the market.

4. Social Media and Online Behavior

Your target audience regularly communicates their demands and preferences online. Monitor social media platforms, internet forums, and review sites to obtain information. Pay attention to:

• feelings: Analyze the feelings and emotions expressed in talks about your business or specialty.

• Product or Service suggestions: Look for product suggestions and endorsements made by your target clients.

• Online groups: Identify relevant online groups or forums where your audience congregates to discuss relevant issues.

5. Observe and Analyze

Observational research entails actually viewing your target audience in their natural habitat. Consider performing field research or ethnographic studies to examine their behavior, requirements, and pain spots. Pay attention to:

• Behavior Patterns: Document common behavior patterns, such as purchasing habits or product use.

• Pain Points: Observe the issues individuals confront in their everyday lives that your company can solve.

• Consumer Journey: Map out the phases of their consumer journey, from issue detection to purchasing choices.

6. Online Analytics

Leverage internet analytics technologies to acquire insights into the online activity of your prospective consumers. These tools can offer data on:

• Website Traffic: Analyze the traffic to your website or related platforms to discover visitor demographics and habits.

• User Pathways: Track how users travel through your online content or items to find spots of interest or drop-offs.

• Conversion Funnel: Examine the conversion funnel to discover when consumers perform desired actions or exit the process.

7. Customer Surveys and Feedback

If your firm has already started, collect feedback from current clients. Their insights may help you enhance your company strategy and connect it with their demands. Collect data on:

• happiness Levels: Gauge client happiness with your goods or services.

• Improvement comments: Ask for comments and areas where they feel your organization may improve.

• Loyalty and Retention: Understand what elements contribute to consumer loyalty and retention.

8. Competitor Analysis

Analyze the current items or services that appeal to your target demographic. Understand what your rivals provide, their strengths and flaws, and how your organization may distinguish itself. Key elements to consider include:

• Competitor items: Assess the quality, features, and price of items or services comparable to yours.

• Customer Reviews: Read customer reviews and comments on competing products to uncover consumer pain areas.

• Market Gaps: Identify areas where rivals may not completely match the demands or wants of your audience.

9. Feedback Integration

Regularly incorporate consumer feedback and insights into your company plan. Create a feedback loop to guarantee that your firm consistently changes to the changing demands and preferences of your target audience.

10. Test and Iterate

Once you've obtained a solid grasp of your target audience, employ this information to develop your company concept. Create prototypes or minimum viable products (MVPs) and test them with your audience. Use their comments to tweak and enhance your offers.

By completely knowing your target audience, you'll be better positioned to build a product or service that connects with their requirements and preferences. This insight will drive your marketing efforts and the entire company strategy. In the following chapters, we'll examine how to apply this information to establish a sound business strategy and develop tactics for reaching and engaging your target audience successfully.

5

BUSINESS PLANNING BASICS

The Importance of a Business Plan

A business plan is frequently regarded as the blueprint for your entrepreneurial career. It's a thorough document that details your company objectives, strategy, and financial predictions. While some entrepreneurs may be tempted to skip this phase, recognizing the value of a business plan is important to your venture's success.

1. Clarity and Direction

A business strategy offers you with clarity and direction. It requires you to establish your company goals, objectives, and strategies systematically. By putting your thoughts on paper, you establish a clear route to follow. This clarity is crucial for you as the company owner and for your staff.

2. Goal Setting and Tracking

A business plan helps you create quantifiable goals and objectives. These objectives act as standards for your business's success. By measuring your success against the targets specified in your plan, you can determine where you're succeeding and where you may need to change your approach.

3. Communication Tool

Your company plan is not only for internal use; it also functions as a communication tool. When seeking capital from investors, loans from banks, or collaborations with other organizations, a well-structured plan helps explain your vision and strategy successfully. It communicates to people that you've thought critically about your company.

4. Decision Making

A company strategy may be your compass while making key choices. if you're exploring a new marketing approach, expanding into new areas, or recruiting extra personnel, your plan gives a reference point for analyzing if each move matches your overall goals.

5. Risk Assessment

Entrepreneurship comes with inherent hazards, but a business plan helps you to identify possible risks and build mitigation techniques. By thinking through probable problems and setbacks in advance, you'll be more equipped to manage them when they come.

6. Financial Management

Your company plan comprises financial estimates and a budget. This financial blueprint aids you in managing your funds properly. It helps you estimate cash flow requirements, develop pricing strategies, and make educated financial choices.

7. Attracting Investors

Investors, whether they be angel investors, venture capitalists, or lenders, frequently want a business plan as a requirement for granting funds. A well-prepared strategy not only indicates your devotion but also offers investors a clear knowledge of the prospective return on their investment.

8. Realistic Expectations

Through the process of producing a business plan, you'll do market research, analyze your competition, and examine your financial requirements. This study will help you establish reasonable expectations about your business's potential and the problems you may experience.

9. Continuous Improvement

Your business plan is not set in stone; it's a dynamic document that may develop as your firm evolves. Regularly examining and revising your strategy helps you to adjust to changing market circumstances, rising opportunities, and new problems.

10. Credibility

Having a well-structured business plan provides legitimacy to your firm. It indicates to stakeholders, partners, and customers that you take your company seriously and have a well-thought-out plan.

In conclusion, a business plan is a vital tool for any entrepreneur. It delivers clarity, informs decision-making, attracts investors, and helps you anticipate and reduce risks. With a sound business plan in place, you'll be better equipped to negotiate the hurdles of entrepreneurship and strive toward the success of your firm. In the following chapters, we'll examine the components of a business plan in depth and help you through the process of constructing one that matches your specific company.

Components of a Solid Business Plan

Creating a business plan entails arranging your ideas, objectives, and strategies into a document that gives a clear and thorough picture of your firm. A strong business strategy often comprises the following critical components:

1. Executive Summary

The executive summary is a succinct review of your whole business strategy. It should quickly explain your firm, emphasize its unique selling offer, and give a glimpse of your financial expectations.

While it appears at the beginning of the plan, it is generally written last, after you've finished the other parts.

2. Business Description

This section gives a full description of your company, including:

• Your business's purpose and vision.

• The issue your business solves or the demand it meets.

• Your unique value proposition and what sets your firm distinct from the competition.

• The legal form of your company (e.g., sole proprietorship, LLC, corporation).

3. Market Analysis

The market analysis section investigates your target market and industry. It includes:

• Research on your target audience, including demographics, psychographics, and behavior.

• An evaluation of your industry, its size, growth, and trends.

• Competitor analysis, emphasizing their strengths and flaws.

• Your positioning within the market and tactics for reaching your target audience.

4. Organizational Structure

This section covers your business's internal structure, including:

• The roles and duties of important team members.

• An organizational chart displaying the hierarchy and reporting structure.

• Information on any strategic partners or advisers.

5. Product or Service Description

Here, you submit specific information on the items or services your firm provides, including:

• Features and advantages of your goods or services.

• The issue they address or the demand they satisfy.

• Any intellectual property or proprietary technology linked with them.

• The development and manufacturing process, if relevant.

6. Marketing and Sales Strategies

This section discusses your strategy for promoting and selling your goods or services:

• Your marketing strategy, including online and offline techniques.

• Sales techniques, such as price, distribution, and sales channels.

• Your sales and customer acquisition process.

7. Financial Projections

This is a vital component of your business strategy and includes:

• Revenue predictions for the first several years of your firm.

• Expense projections, including starting expenditures and continuous operational expenses.

• Cash flow predictions to manage your money properly.

• Break-even analysis to identify when your firm will become profitable.

8. Funding Request (if appropriate)

If you're seeking external money, this section discusses your financial needs:

• The amount of funds necessary and its purpose.

• How you intend to utilize the money and why they are essential.

• Your repayment schedule and any collateral you may supply.

9. Risk Assessment

Identify and evaluate the risks and problems your firm may encounter, and identify methods to manage these risks.

10. Implementation Plan

Detail the measures you will take to begin and expand your firm, including a timeframe, milestones, and responsibilities.

11. Appendix

Include any other papers or facts that support your business strategy, such as:

• Resumes of important team members.

• Market research data and analysis.

• Letters of intent from possible partners or consumers.

• Legal papers, licenses, or permissions.

Remember that a business plan is not a static document. It should be examined and modified often as your company develops. A well-structured business plan acts as a blueprint for your firm, helping you remain on course and adapt to changing conditions. In the following chapters, we'll lead you through the process of constructing each of these components in depth to produce a robust and thorough business plan.

6

FINANCIAL PLANNING

Creating a Startup Budget

One of the key elements in turning your company concept into a reality is generating a startup budget. A well-thought-out budget not only helps you understand your early financial needs but also establishes the framework for good financial management throughout your company journey.

1. Start with a Detailed Revenue Projection

Begin your beginning budget by calculating your revenue. Consider your price approach, the number of clients you hope to target, and any other sources of revenue. Be realistic in your estimates, and examine both best-case and worst-case possibilities.

2. Identify Initial Startup Costs

List all the expenditures you'll pay while beginning your company. This might include:

• One-time Costs: Expenses include establishing your firm, acquiring permissions, and buying initial inventory or equipment.

• Ongoing Costs: Monthly expenditures including rent, electricity, insurance, and marketing.

• Employee salary: If you intend to recruit staff, mention their salary and benefits.

• Marketing and Advertising: Budget for marketing activities to attract your early consumers.

• technologies and Software: Costs related to software, hardware, and other technologies.

• Legal and Accounting expenses: Include expenses for legal and accounting services.

• Loan or Interest installments: If you've acquired a business loan, account for the monthly installments.

3. Estimate Operating Expenses

Operating expenditures are the charges connected with operating your firm. These include continuing expenditures like rent, electricity, insurance, and marketing. When assessing operational expenses:

• Consider both fixed and variable expenses. Fixed costs (e.g., rent) stay constant, whereas variable expenses (e.g., utilities) may fluctuate.

• Research industry standards to discover what comparable organizations spend on operational expenditures.

• Be cautious in your projections to accommodate for unanticipated expenditures.

4. Account for Cash Reserves

It's crucial to keep financial reserves to meet unanticipated costs or times of decreased earnings. A general rule of thumb is to have three to six months' worth of operational expenditures put aside as a buffer.

5. Track One-Time Expenses

Startup enterprises generally have one-time expenditures that may not repeat in the same manner. These may include:

• Costs associated with putting up a physical site.

• Licensing and permissions.

• Initial marketing and advertising initiatives.

• Website development and branding.

6. Consider Debt Financing

If you want to employ debt financing, such as a company loan, include the monthly installments in your budget. Factor in the interest rates and the period of the loan.

7. Review and Revise

A startup budget is a dynamic document that should be examined and amended constantly. As your company evolves, your financial demands and circumstances may change. Ensure that your budget is a flexible instrument that can adjust to developing situations.

8. Seek Professional Advice

If you're confused about generating your startup budget, try obtaining guidance from a financial counselor or accountant. They can give help and ensure that your budget is thorough and precise.

9. Use Budgeting Tools

Numerous budgeting tools and software are available to help you design and manage your startup budget. These tools help speed the procedure and give a clear snapshot of your financial status.

10. Be Prepared for Contingencies

In your budget, incorporate a contingency reserve for unforeseen spending or changes in your business's financial picture. This cushion may bring peace of mind and financial security during hard times.

A well-crafted startup budget is a great resource for directing your business's financial choices and ensuring you're appropriately prepared for the difficulties and possibilities that lie ahead. In the coming chapters, we'll cover financial planning in greater depth, including making thorough financial plans and understanding cash flow management.

Forecasting Revenue and Expenses

Forecasting income and costs is a vital component of financial planning for any business. By developing precise estimates, you can anticipate your financial demands and guarantee that your organization stays financially healthy as it expands. Here's how to anticipate your income and costs effectively:

1. Revenue Forecasting

Revenue forecasting entails calculating the money your organization will make over a set time, generally on a monthly or annual basis. To construct an accurate revenue forecast:

• Market Research: Base your projections on rigorous market research and a strong grasp of your target audience and industry.

• Pricing Strategy: Consider your pricing strategy and the rates your consumers are willing to pay for your goods or services.

• Sales Projections: Project your sales based on the amount of products or services you plan to sell and the predicted client demand.

• Seasonal Variation: If your firm sees seasonal swings, account for this in your predictions.

• Growth Projections: Factor in predicted growth as your firm develops and recruit's new clients.

• Customer Retention: Consider the lifetime worth of your customers and how long you intend to keep them.

2. Expense Forecasting

Expense forecasting entails predicting the expenses connected with operating your firm. This comprises both one-time setup fees and continuing running expenses. To construct an accurate spending forecast:

• Start with a List: Create a detailed list of all prospective expenditures, including fixed and variable prices.

• Vendor estimates: Obtain estimates from suppliers and vendors to assess the prices of items or services you'll need.

• Research: Research industry benchmarks to determine what comparable organizations spend on operational expenditures.

• Legal and Compliance: Ensure you've accounted for any legal or compliance-related charges.

• Loan Payments: Include any monthly payments for business loans or funding.

• Employee Expenses: If you want to recruit staff, budget for their pay and benefits.

• Contingency reserve: Include a contingency reserve for unforeseen costs.

3. Cash Flow Forecasting

Cash flow forecasting is vital for ensuring your organization has adequate cash to meet its costs. It entails monitoring the movement of money into and out of your firm over a specified time. To generate an accurate cash flow forecast:

• Starting Cash: Begin with your original cash balance or starting money.

• Inflows: Estimate the cash flowing into your firm from sources like sales, loans, or investments.

• Outflows: Estimate the cash coming out of your firm for costs like salary, rent, and inventory purchases.

• Contingency: Include a contingency for unanticipated costs or volatility in cash flow.

• evaluate Periodically: Regularly evaluate and update your cash flow projection to ensure it matches the current financial status of your firm.

4. Sensitivity Analysis

Incorporate sensitivity analysis into your financial planning. This entails examining numerous possibilities that might affect your income and costs. For example:

• Best-case situation: A situation in which your firm performs incredibly well.

• Worst-case situation: A situation in which your firm encounters obstacles, such as lower-than-expected sales or additional expenses.

• Realistic Scenario: A scenario that offers your best assessment of how your firm will function.

By studying these situations, you may prepare for possible financial outcomes and make educated choices.

5. Periodic Review

Regularly examine and revise your income and spending predictions. As your firm develops, your financial assumptions may vary. Periodic evaluation ensures that your financial planning stays precise and current.

6. Seek Professional Guidance

If you're hesitant about producing realistic financial projections, try obtaining advice from a financial counselor or accountant. They may give significant insights and guarantee that your estimates are reasonable and realistic.

Creating solid income and spending estimates is a critical element of financial planning. Accurate projections help you make educated financial choices and guarantee that your organization has the required resources to prosper and weather unforeseen problems. In the next chapters, we'll look further into issues such as cash flow management and financial reporting.

7

CHOOSING A LEGAL STRUCTURE

Types of Business Structures: Sole Proprietorship, LLC, Corporation

Choosing the correct legal structure for your firm is a significant choice that may affect your responsibility, taxes, and operational flexibility. There are various popular company structures, each having its merits and downsides. In this chapter, we'll study the most typical business structures: sole proprietorship, limited liability company (LLC), and corporation.

1. Sole Proprietorship

Advantages:

• Simplicity: Sole proprietorships are uncomplicated to establish and administer.

• Complete Control: You have complete control over corporate choices and activities.

• Tax Benefits: Business revenue is disclosed on your tax return, simplifying taxes.

Disadvantages:

• Unlimited Liability: You are personally accountable for corporate debts and liabilities.

• Limited Access to Capital: It may be tough to get finance or attract investors.

• restricted Growth: Growth potential is frequently restricted compared to other structures.

Best for:

Sole proprietorships are appropriate for small firms with little risk, minimum investment, and a single owner who desires total control.

2. Limited Liability Company (LLC)

Advantages:

• Limited Liability: Owners' assets are safeguarded from corporate debts and litigation.

• Tax Flexibility: An LLC may select how it is taxed, either as a sole proprietorship, partnership, S corporation, or C corporation.

• Simplified Formalities: Fewer administrative obligations compared to corporations.

Disadvantages:

• Limited Life: An LLC may have a limited life, depending on state rules.

• Complexity: Compliance standards might vary by state, and tax ramifications can be extensive.

• Limited Access to Capital: Attracting investors might be more problematic compared to businesses.

Best for:

LLCs are excellent for small to medium-sized firms searching for liability protection and flexibility in taxes.

3. Corporation

Advantages:

• Limited Liability: Shareholders are not individually accountable for corporate debts and legal concerns.

• Perpetual Existence: A company may continue to exist beyond the lives of its founders.

• Easier funds Raising: Easier access to funds via the selling of stocks and recruiting investors.

Disadvantages:

• Complex Administration: Corporations need formal administrative processes, including shareholder meetings and rigorous record-keeping.

• Double taxes: C companies may incur double taxes (corporate and individual) on profits.

• rules: Corporations are subject to different rules and compliance obligations.

Best for:

Corporations are appropriate for firms with considerable development potential, many owners, and the need to attract major investments.

4. Choosing the Right Structure

The choice of a legal structure relies on your company objectives, amount of risk, and long-term intentions. Here are some factors to help you decide:

• Liability Protection: If you require personal asset protection, an LLC or company may be preferred.

• Taxation: Consider the taxation alternatives available with each structure and which match your financial objectives.

• Ownership and Management: Determine how you want to arrange ownership and management.

• Development Plans: Consider your development potential and availability of money. Corporations are frequently better equipped for large expansion.

• Compliance and Administrative Requirements: Be aware of the administrative obligations and regulatory requirements connected with each structure.

• Exit Strategy: Your long-term intentions and prospective exit strategies, such as selling the firm or going public, should also affect your decision.

Choosing the correct legal structure is a crucial choice that may affect your business's legal, financial, and operational aspects. It's recommended to speak with legal and financial specialists to ensure you pick the structure that matches your individual company goals and objectives. In the next chapters, we'll examine the legal and financial aspects further, including the procedure of registering your firm.

Legal and Tax Implications of Each Structure

Selecting the correct legal structure for your company includes analyzing not just the benefits but also the legal and tax concerns connected with each form. Here, we'll discuss the important legal and tax concerns for the three typical business structures: sole proprietorship, limited liability company (LLC), and corporation.

1. Sole Proprietorship

Legal Implications:

• Personal Liability: In a single proprietorship, there is no legal distinction between you and your company. This implies you have limitless personal accountability for corporate debts and legal proceedings. Your assets are in danger.

• Regulations: Sole proprietorships frequently have fewer regulatory obligations and formalities compared to other arrangements, making them easier to handle.

Tax Implications:

• Pass-Through Taxation: In a sole proprietorship, company revenue is normally recorded on your tax return. These "pass-through" taxes streamline the tax procedure.

• Self-Employment Tax: As a single owner, you are responsible for paying self-employment tax, which includes Social Security and Medicare payments.

2. Limited Liability Company (LLC)

Legal Implications:

• Limited responsibility: An LLC gives protection to its owners (members) by limiting their responsibility. In most circumstances, members are not personally accountable for corporate debts or legal proceedings.

• Operating Agreement: While an operating agreement is not usually legally needed, drafting one may assist in defining how the LLC will be administered and how profits and losses will be allocated.

Tax Implications:

• Tax freedom: LLCs have freedom in how they are taxed. By default, they are taxed as pass-through businesses, comparable to sole proprietorships and partnerships. However, an LLC may opt to be taxed as an S company or a C corporation, depending on its tax goals.

• Self-Employment Tax: Members of an LLC who are actively engaged in the company may be liable to self-employment tax on their portion of the earnings.

3. Corporation

Legal Implications:

• Limited Liability: Corporations give a high degree of personal liability protection for stockholders. Shareholders are typically not directly accountable for firm debts or legal actions.

• sophisticated Formalities: Corporations have more sophisticated administrative and formal obligations. These include having frequent shareholder meetings, keeping accurate records, and following certain rules.

Tax Implications:

• C Corporation Taxation: C corporations are subject to double taxation. They are taxed at the corporate level on earnings, and shareholders are subsequently taxed on any dividends paid. However, C companies have the benefit of being able to deduct many company expenditures.

• S Corporation taxes: S companies, although subject to various limitations, allow pass-through taxes, comparable to sole proprietorships and LLCs. This implies that income and losses are declared on shareholders' tax returns.

• Tax Credits and Deductions: Depending on the corporation's industry and operations, there may be chances to obtain different tax credits and deductions.

4. Legal and Tax Implications: Considerations

When establishing a legal form for your firm, here are some crucial considerations for the legal and tax implications:

• Personal Liability: Evaluate how much personal liability protection you need. If you wish to preserve your assets, entities like LLCs and corporations may be better.

• Tax goals: Determine your tax goals and analyze the tax consequences of each structure. Each structure has distinct tax treatment.

• Regulations and Compliance: Be aware of the administrative and regulatory obligations connected with each structure. Corporations often have greater formality and compliance duties.

• Ownership and Management: Consider how you want to arrange ownership and management. Sole proprietorships allow total control, whereas corporations have a board of directors and stockholders.

• expansion and Financing: If you expect considerable expansion and the need for outside investment, companies may be ideal for recruiting investors.

Choosing the correct legal structure is a difficult issue that should coincide with your company's objectives and strategies. It's recommended to contact legal and tax specialists to ensure you pick the structure that best matches your company objectives while reducing legal and tax concerns. In the following chapters, we'll cover the process of registering your selected company form and understanding financial duties in greater depth.

8

FUNDING YOUR BUSINESS

Funding Options: Self-Funding, Loans, Investors

Securing the required cash to start and expand your firm is a critical step for every entrepreneur. Understanding the many financing sources available is vital to making educated financial choices. In this chapter, we'll discuss the three basic financing options: self-funding, loans, and investors.

1. Self-Funding

Advantages:

• Complete Control: When you self-fund your firm, you keep complete control over all choices, since you are not beholden to investors or lenders.

• Minimal Debt: Self-funding avoids the need to take on debt, avoiding interest payments and long-term financial responsibilities.

• Flexibility: You may adjust your company plans and pivot without having to seek or get permission from other parties.

Disadvantages:

• Limited Resources: Your finances and resources may be inadequate for considerable development or expansion.

• Personal Risk: Self-funding might expose your assets to company losses and liabilities.

• Slow Growth: Self-funding may restrict the rate at which your organization may develop since it depends on your resources.

Best for:

Self-funding is a fantastic alternative for firms with minimal capital needs, low-risk initiatives, and entrepreneurs who wish to keep complete control and limit financial responsibilities.

2. Loans

Advantages:

• Access to funds: Loans give access to extra funds, allowing your firm to finance growth, inventory, equipment, or other requirements.

• Spread Out Payments: Loan repayments may be scheduled over time, lessening the immediate financial impact.

• Potential for Growth: Loans may offer growth potential that would not be feasible via self-funding alone.

Disadvantages:

• Interest Costs: Borrowing money often requires paying interest, which adds to the total cost of the loan.

• Debt commitments: Loans generate financial commitments that need to be addressed, possibly hurting your business's cash flow.

• Qualification Requirements: Securing a loan may be competitive and may demand a solid credit history, collateral, or a proven company track record.

Best for:

Loans are a great alternative for firms to have a clear plan for utilizing the cash and a method for repaying the loan. They are often utilized for working capital, equipment acquisition, or expansion activities.

3. Investors

Advantages:

• Significant funds: Investors, such as angel investors or venture capitalists, may give large funds to your organization, allowing quick development and expansion.

• experience and Resources: Some investors provide substantial industry experience, contacts, and resources to help your firm.

• Shared Risk: Investors share the financial risk and give help in addressing obstacles and opportunities.

Disadvantages:

• Loss of influence: Depending on the conditions of the investment, you may need to cede some degree of influence over your firm and its choices.

• portion of Profits: Investors often anticipate a portion of the profits or equity in return for their funding, which might affect their ownership position.

• High Expectations: Investors generally have high expectations for corporate success and may push for aggressive expansion, which may increase pressure.

Best for:

Investors are a fantastic alternative for organizations with strong growth potential, scalability, and a clear route to success. They are frequent in technological companies and enterprises that need large money for growth.

4. Choosing the Right Funding Option

Selecting the proper financing choice relies on your business's individual requirements, objectives, and financial status. Consider the following factors:

• money Requirements: Assess how much money your firm requires to fulfill its goals.

• Risk Tolerance: Evaluate your risk tolerance and how comfortable you are with personal financial exposure.

• Ownership and Control: Determine how much ownership and control you are prepared to give to outside investors.

• development and Profitability: Consider your business's potential for development and profitability and how each financing choice corresponds with your growth plan.

• Utilization of money: Be clear on how you plan to utilize the money and if it will help your business's success.

• Long-Term Vision: Align your financing decision with your long-term vision for the firm, including possible exit alternatives.

• Financial Planning: Ensure you have a sound financial strategy in place, whether you are self-funding, borrowing, or seeking investment.

It's recommended to talk with financial consultants and examine different financing possibilities before making a choice. Each alternative has its merits and cons, and the optimal decision will rely on your company's conditions and goals. In the next chapters, we'll get into the mechanics of obtaining funds, creating loan applications, and courting investors.

Securing Startup Capital

Securing startup money is a critical milestone for your organization, and it frequently demands a smart strategy. Here are measures to assist you in getting the required funding to establish or develop your business:

1. Self-Funding

own resources: Consider utilizing your resources as a source of beginning cash. This indicates your devotion to the company and might help you keep complete control.

Bootstrapping: Operate your firm with minimum outside investment and an emphasis on producing money from day one. This technique may lessen your dependency on external financing.

house Equity: If you own a house, you may leverage your home equity via a home equity loan or line of credit.

2. Loans

Bank Loans: Traditional bank loans are a frequent source of finance for small enterprises. To receive a bank loan, you normally need a sound business plan, a decent credit history, and collateral in certain situations.

Small Business Administration (SBA) Loans: The SBA provides numerous loan programs that may give cheap financing solutions for small enterprises. These loans are typically more accessible to entrepreneurs who may not qualify for standard bank loans.

Online Lenders: Online lenders and peer-to-peer lending platforms may be more flexible and have speedier approval procedures. Be prepared to present precise financial details and have a well-structured business strategy.

3. Investors

Angel Investors: Angel investors are people who offer financing to entrepreneurs in return for stock ownership. They typically provide industry experience and beneficial contacts.

Venture Capitalists (VCs): Venture capitalists are professional investors who manage funds to invest in high-growth enterprises. Securing venture funding often entails a difficult procedure and frequently needs to prove large growth potential.

Crowdfunding: Crowdfunding systems enable you to raise funds from a wide spectrum of individual investors, generally via online campaigns. This method may be useful for certain sorts of companies and goods.

Pitch contests and Contests: Many organizations and events organize pitch contests where entrepreneurs may present their company ideas and perhaps earn investment.

4. Grants and Competitions

Government Grants: Research government grants and incentives available for small enterprises. These funds generally have particular qualifying conditions, and the application procedure might be competitive.

Private Grants: Some private organizations and charities make grants to help enterprises in certain sectors or with special social or environmental aims.

Business contests: Many institutions and organizations conduct business plan contests where you may win funds to launch your firm.

5. Family and Friends

Consider obtaining financial help from family members or close friends who believe in your company concept. Ensure that any such agreements are well-documented and explicit to prevent any pressures on personal ties.

6. Strategic Partnerships

Collaborate with strategic partners who can give not just finance but also knowledge, resources, or access to markets. These relationships may be mutually advantageous for both sides.

7. Preparation and Documentation

No matter the source of your startup money, it's vital to be well-prepared. This includes:

• Develop a detailed business plan that explains your company concept, income predictions, and the planned use of cash.

• Maintaining excellent financial records and exhibiting a comprehensive awareness of your business's financial health.

• Building a great pitch and presentation to attract possible investors or lenders.

• Consulting with financial consultants or mentors to enhance your finance plan and approach.

8. Legal and Financial Due Diligence

Ensure you are well-versed in the legal and financial ramifications of any financing arrangement. Consult with legal and financial specialists to evaluate agreements and understand your duties.

Securing startup finance is a critical milestone on your business path. It involves careful preparation, a great pitch, and an awareness of the many financing sources accessible. Tailor your strategy to your firm's particular requirements, and be persistent in your attempts to raise the required financing to transform your business concept into a profitable reality. In the next chapters, we'll discuss further specifics regarding drafting loan applications, obtaining investors, and managing your business's finances successfully.

9

REGISTERING YOUR BUSINESS

Legal Requirements and Permits

When you decide to establish a company, one of the first crucial actions is to register your firm and secure the appropriate permissions and licenses. Meeting legal standards is vital to ensure your firm runs within the law and avoids possible complications. Here's what you need to consider while registering your company and acquiring permits:

1. Business Structure and Name

Choose a Legal Structure: Decide on the legal structure for your firm, whether it's a sole proprietorship, LLC, corporation, or another form. Your decision impacts the registration procedure and your responsibility.

Business Name: Select a distinctive and legally compatible business name. Check for trademark disputes and check the name conforms with your state's naming standards.

2. Register with the Appropriate Authorities

Business Entity Registration: Register your business entity with the proper state and municipal authorities. This frequently entails submitting articles of incorporation or organization, depending on your company form.

Employer Identification Number (EIN): Obtain an EIN from the IRS if your firm has workers or operates as a corporation or partnership. This number is used for tax reasons.

company Licenses: Identify the precise licenses and permissions necessary for your sort of company. The kinds and amount of licenses required might vary greatly based on your region, industry, and the nature of your company operations.

Sales Tax Permit: If your company includes selling items or services, you may need a sales tax permit to collect and return sales tax to your state.

Health and Safety Permits: Depending on your industry, you may need health department permits, fire department licenses, or other safety-related permissions to guarantee your firm satisfies certain health and safety requirements.

3. Local Regulations

Local Zoning Laws: Check local zoning rules to check whether your company site conforms with zoning laws. Zoning regulations influence how and where companies may operate inside a municipality.

Home-based company legislation: If you want to operate a home-based company, check you comply with any home business legislation in your region.

signs and Advertising Requirements: Some local authorities have requirements governing signs and advertising, so be careful to grasp these limits.

4. Federal Regulations

business-certain requirements: Depending on your business, you may need to comply with certain federal requirements. This is frequent in industries such as healthcare, finance, and food service.

Import/Export restrictions: If your firm includes foreign commerce, be aware of import and export restrictions and secure the relevant permissions and licenses.

Environmental rules: Certain enterprises may be subject to environmental rules. Ensure compliance with legislation about waste disposal, emissions, and other environmental problems.

5. Professional Licensing

Professional Licensing: If your company includes delivering professional services, you may require a professional license. This applies to areas such as law, medicine, and accountancy.

Trade and Occupational Licenses: Some sectors need trade or occupational licenses. For example, contractors and electricians frequently require particular licenses.

6. Application Process

Application prerequisites: Understand the prerequisites for each permit or license you need. This may require submitting specified paperwork, paying fees, and undertaking inspections.

Application Timeline: Be mindful of the time it takes to process applications. Start this step early to minimize delays in launching your company.

7. Compliance and Renewals

Ongoing Compliance: Maintain compliance with all relevant rules, permits, and licenses throughout your company activities. Failure to do so might result in fines, penalties, or even company closure.

Renewals: Many permits and licenses need renewal at regular periods. Stay prepared and ensure you renew them on schedule.

8. Seek Legal and Professional Guidance

Seek legal and professional help to manage the registration and permitting procedure. An attorney, accountant, or business consultant may give vital help to ensure you satisfy all legal requirements.

Registering your company and securing the relevant permissions and licenses is a vital step in creating a legally compliant and flourishing organization. It's crucial to investigate and understand your unique obligations and communicate with the necessary authorities to ensure your company functions smoothly and in full compliance with the law. In the coming chapters, we'll discuss various elements of starting up your company, including picking a location and setting up your office.

Registering Your Business Name

Your company name is a vital component of your brand identification, and registering it is important to safeguard your rights and operate lawfully. Here's how to go about registering your company name:

1. Choose a Unique Business Name

Select a distinctive and recognizable name for your company. Ensure it's not currently in use by another company, and it doesn't infringe on trademarks or copyrights. The name should represent your brand and be memorable to your target audience.

2. Legal Structure and Name Rules

Consider the legal structure of your company, since this might affect your business name. Some rules to bear in mind:

• solo Proprietorship: If you're operating as a sole proprietor, you may use your name for your firm or adopt a "doing business as" (DBA) name.

• LLC or Corporation: If you've created an LLC or corporation, your company name must conform with state naming requirements, which sometimes include incorporating phrases like "LLC" or "Inc." in the name.

• Trademark Considerations: Before registering your name, check for trademark disputes. The U.S. Patent and Trademark Office (USPTO) website is a helpful resource for this purpose.

3. Register Your Business Name

The particular procedure for registering your company name differs by area. Here are general steps to follow:

• State Registration: In most circumstances, you'll register your company name with the relevant state agency. This is frequently the Secretary of State's office. You may need to register a "Doing Business as" (DBA) or fake business name registration.

• Federal Trademark: If you want to use your company name nationally or internationally, you may register it as a federal trademark with the USPTO. This grants legal protection and exclusive rights to the name.

4. Renewals and Maintenance

After registering your company name, be aware of any renewal or maintenance obligations. Some states demand periodic renewals, while federal trademarks require maintenance filings to keep the registration alive.

5. Notify the Public

Make your company name public by utilizing it in your marketing materials, on your website, and in your business communications. This helps develop your brand and improves brand awareness.

6. Protect Your Business Name

Once your company name is registered, take actions to safeguard it:

• Monitor for Infringements: Keep a watch out for any unlawful use of your company name by others, and take appropriate legal action if required.

• Defend Your Trademark: If you've registered your company name as a trademark, be prepared to defend it in case of trademark disputes.

7. Seek Professional Advice

Consider getting legal guidance to verify your company name is legally compliant and sufficiently protected. An attorney with knowledge of intellectual property and corporate law may give important counsel.

8. Internet Domain Name

If you want to establish an online presence, consider acquiring a domain name that matches your company name. This helps with brand consistency and internet presence.

9. Brand Identity

Ensure that your company name corresponds with your entire brand concept. It should represent your business's beliefs, goods, and services, and connect with your target audience.

10. Consistency in Marketing

Consistently utilize your registered company name in all marketing materials, including websites, business cards, and social media accounts. This enhances brand identification and strengthens your brand identity.

Registering your company name is a key step in creating your brand identification and legally preserving your rights. It's a procedure that demands careful study and compliance with both state and federal standards. By completing these measures, you can guarantee that your company name not only expresses your brand successfully but also stands up to legal examination. In the next chapters, we'll go more into building up your company, including picking a location and setting up your office.

10

LOCATION AND WORKSPACE

Choosing a Business Location

Selecting the correct company location is a key choice that may substantially affect the success of your firm. The site you pick may affect accessibility, visibility, expenses, and your ability to attract consumers and staff. Here's how to go about finding the proper company location:

1. Define Your Needs

Begin by determining your unique demands and objectives for a company site. Consider considerations such as:

• Target Audience: Where is your target audience situated, and what venues are convenient for them?

• industrial: Does your firm need closeness to certain suppliers, partners, or industrial clusters?

• Accessibility: Is the location conveniently accessible for consumers, staff, and suppliers? Consider concerns like transit and parking.

• Competition: Are there rivals in the region, and how can they influence your business?

• expenses: What are the expenses involved with operating in a given area, including rent, utilities, and taxes?

• rules: Consider local rules and zoning restrictions that may affect your company operations.

2. Research Potential Locations

Once you've determined your requirements, start exploring suitable places. Consider variables like:

• Demographics: Study the demographics of the region, including population, income levels, and age groupings. This information may assist you in understanding your possible client base.

• Foot Traffic: Assess the amount of foot traffic in the region. High foot traffic may be good for retail enterprises.

• Competitive Landscape: Understand the competitors in the region. Are there comparable enterprises nearby, and how do you aim to separate yourself?

• Zoning and permissions: Check local zoning restrictions and permissions to guarantee your company operations are authorized in the selected site.

• Accessibility: Evaluate transportation choices and accessibility for both consumers and staff. Proximity to major highways, public transit, and parking facilities might be vital.

3. Consider Costs

Evaluate the expenses associated with each prospective site. This includes:

• Rent or Lease Costs: Determine the cost of leasing or renting space in each location. Consider the conditions and any future rent hikes.

• Utility Costs: Understand the cost of utilities, such as power, water, and internet services.

• Taxes and Fees: Research local taxes and fees that may apply to your company, including property taxes and business licenses.

• Maintenance and Upkeep: Consider any maintenance or remodeling charges necessary to make the facility appropriate for your company.

4. Evaluate Growth Potential

Assess the development potential of each place. Consider considerations such as:

• Market Trends: Research market trends and growth estimates for the sector to assess whether they correspond with your long-term company objectives.

• Future projects: Find out about any impending projects or changes in the region that might affect your company.

• Space Scalability: Ensure that the space you pick can allow possible growth and development.

5. Test the Location

If feasible, try evaluating the site before committing to a long-term lease. You may achieve this in ways like:

• Pop-Up Shops: Set up a short pop-up store or a test site to measure client interest and demand.

• Market Research: Conduct market research and surveys to get input from prospective consumers in the region.

• Competitor Analysis: Study the accomplishments and problems of rivals in the same place.

6. Seek Expert Advice

Consider working with a commercial real estate agent who specializes in the region. They may give significant insights and assist you in identifying appropriate homes that fulfill your demands.

7. Negotiate Lease Terms

When you've chosen a place that fulfills your requirements, negotiate lease terms that are suitable for your firm. Pay attention to aspects like lease terms, rent hikes, and any included facilities or services.

8. Legal and Regulatory Compliance

Ensure you comply with all legal and regulatory standards for the selected region. This involves getting all appropriate permissions and licenses.

Choosing the ideal company location is a crucial choice that demands considerable study and analysis. It's crucial to balance your company's demands with elements like accessibility, expenses, and development potential. By following these procedures and receiving professional help when required, you can make an educated choice that puts your company up for success. In the next chapters, we'll study how to set up your workspace and establish an efficient working environment.

Setting Up Your Workspace

Once you've found the perfect company location, the following step is to set up your office successfully. Your workplace plays a critical influence on your business's productivity, functioning, and overall success. Here's how you go about setting up your workspace:

1. Assess Your Needs

Before you start setting up your workstation, consider your demands and expectations. Consider considerations such as:

• Space Requirements: Determine the amount of space you require for your company activities, including workstations, equipment, and storage.

• Furniture and Equipment: Make a list of the essential furniture and equipment, such as desks, chairs, computers, printers, and any specialty tools.

• arrangement and Flow: Plan the arrangement of your workstation to facilitate an effective flow of work and cooperation among team members.

• Storage Solutions: Consider storage solutions for papers, supplies, and inventories.

• Comfort and Ergonomics: Pay attention to the comfort and ergonomics of your workstation to improve the well-being and productivity of your staff.

2. Budget and Prioritize

Establish a budget for setting up your workspace. Prioritize vital tasks and distribute funding appropriately. While it's crucial to build a pleasant and functioning office, it's also important to manage expenditures wisely.

3. Furniture and Equipment

Choose proper furnishings and equipment that correspond with your company goals and budget. Consider the following:

• Quality and Durability: Invest in quality furnishings and equipment that will endure, particularly for things that see heavy usage.

• Ergonomics: Select ergonomic furniture to support the health and comfort of your staff. Ergonomic seats and workstations may lessen the incidence of repetitive strain injuries.

• Adaptability: Opt for furniture that can be changed to numerous uses or readily rearranged to fit changing demands.

4. Technology and Connectivity

Ensure that your workplace is outfitted with the required technology and connection. This includes:

• Internet Connection: Establish a stable and high-speed internet connection to assist your company activities.

• gear and Software: Equip your workstations with the gear and software necessary for your unique duties and sector.

• Backup Systems: Implement data backup systems to secure crucial corporate data.

• Security Measures: Invest in cybersecurity measures to defend your digital assets and protect your company from possible dangers.

5. Lighting and Ventilation

Pay attention to the lighting and ventilation at your workplace. Adequate natural and artificial lighting, as well as adequate ventilation, may produce a more pleasant and productive atmosphere.

• Natural Light: Whenever feasible, optimize the usage of natural light in your office. It may increase mood and productivity.

• Artificial Lighting: Install sufficient and adaptable artificial lighting to offer enough illumination for various jobs.

• Ventilation Systems: Ensure that your workstation is well-ventilated to ensure air quality and comfort.

6. Storage Solutions

Consider your storage demands and adopt relevant solutions. This might include file cabinets, shelving, storage closets, or even digital document management solutions.

• Organization: Keep your workstation organized by identifying and classifying things and papers.

• clear: Regularly clear and eliminate superfluous objects to keep a clean and orderly workstation.

7. Personalization

Personalize your workstation to create a good and stimulating environment. This might involve adding artwork, plants, or other features that represent your business culture and values.

8. Health and Safety

Prioritize the health and safety of your staff. Ensure that your workstation conforms with safety requirements and is equipped with required safety measures, like fire extinguishers and first aid kits.

9. Test and Adjust

After setting up your workstation, verify its usefulness and comfort. Be open to making modifications based on input from workers and any recognized areas for improvement.

10. Regular Maintenance

Establish a program for regular maintenance and cleaning to maintain your workstation in excellent shape and foster a productive and pleasant atmosphere.

A well-organized and adequately equipped workstation is vital for the effectiveness and profitability of your organization. It not only generates a nice working atmosphere but also increases productivity and employee happiness. By following these steps, you may establish a workplace that supports your business's objectives and activities. In the next chapters, we'll discuss various parts of operating your firm, including marketing, sales, operations, and growth plans.

11

MARKETING STRATEGIES

Developing a Marketing Plan

A well-thought-out marketing strategy is vital for promoting your company, reaching your target audience, and accomplishing your development objectives. Here's a step-by-step strategy for establishing a successful marketing plan:

1. Define Your Objectives

Start by carefully identifying your marketing goals. What do you hope to accomplish with your marketing efforts? Your aims might include raising brand exposure, generating leads, enhancing revenue, or expanding into new areas.

2. Understand Your Target Audience

To establish a successful marketing strategy, you need a comprehensive grasp of your target demographic. Who are your ideal customers? What are their demographics, preferences, and pain points? Conduct market research and collect data to construct consumer personas.

3. SWOT Analysis

Perform a SWOT (Strengths, Weaknesses, Opportunities, Threats) study of your firm and the market. This study helps you discover internal strengths and weaknesses, as well as external opportunities and dangers that potentially affect your marketing strategy.

4. Define Your Unique Selling Proposition (USP)

Determine what sets your firm distinct from the competition. Your unique selling proposition should be a compelling and distinctive offering that appeals to your target audience.

5. Select Marketing Channels

Choose the marketing methods that are most suited for reaching your audience. Common marketing channels include:

• Online Marketing: Website, social media, email marketing, content marketing, and search engine optimization (SEO).

• Offline Marketing: Print advertising, direct mail, trade exhibitions, and public relations.

• Paid Advertising: Pay-per-click (PPC) advertising, social media advertising, and display advertisements.

6. Set a Budget

Determine your marketing budget. This should be connected with your marketing objectives and the chosen marketing channels. Consider both short-term and long-term costs.

7. Create a Content Plan

Develop a content strategy that describes the sort of material you'll develop, how frequently you'll make it, and where it will be released. Content might include blog entries, social media updates, videos, and more.

8. Marketing Calendar

Establish a marketing calendar to organize and monitor marketing activity. This calendar should contain deadlines for content production, email marketing, and other promotional initiatives.

9. Implement Tracking and Analytics

Set up monitoring and analytics tools to monitor the efficacy of your marketing initiatives. Key performance indicators (KPIs) may include internet traffic, conversion rates, social media engagement, and sales.

10. Marketing Campaigns

Develop unique marketing initiatives that correspond with your goals. These campaigns may concentrate on new debuts, special promotions, or seasonal events. Ensure that each campaign has a clear message and call to action.

11. Marketing Team

Determine who will be accountable for implementing your marketing strategy. If you have a marketing staff, assign roles and duties. If you're a small company owner, consider outsourcing specific jobs or employing freelancers as required.

12. Marketing Materials

Design marketing materials and assets like as brochures, flyers, business cards, and web adverts. Ensure that your branding is consistent across all mediums.

13. Implementation and Testing

Execute your marketing strategy, and be prepared to test and change your techniques. Not all techniques will bring quick results, so be patient and prepared to change as required.

14. Monitor and Measure

Continuously monitor the success of your marketing activities. Use data and analytics to assess the performance of campaigns and adapt your plan appropriately.

15. Review and Optimize

Regularly examine your marketing strategy and make adjustments depending on the insights and data you acquire. Marketing is a constant process, and keeping adaptable and responsive is crucial to long-term success.

16. Stay Informed

Stay current with the newest marketing trends, techniques, and technology. The marketing environment is continuously developing; therefore, ongoing learning is vital.

A well-crafted marketing strategy offers a blueprint for your organization to efficiently reach and engage your target audience. By following these steps and continuously analyzing and updating your plan, you can establish a dynamic marketing strategy that supports your business's growth and success. In the next chapters, we'll go further into particular marketing tactics and approaches to assist you in reaching your marketing objectives.

Online and Offline Marketing Techniques

To establish a well-rounded marketing plan, it's vital to apply a combination of both online and offline marketing strategies. Each strategy has its benefits and may help you reach various groups of your target audience. Here are some successful ways for both:

Online Marketing Techniques

1. Website and SEO (Search Engine Optimization):

• Maintain an informative and user-friendly website.

• Optimize your site for search engines to boost visibility in search results.

• Create useful, relevant material to attract and engage visitors.

2. Social Media Marketing:

• Establish a strong presence on platforms relevant to your target demographic.

• Post consistently with interesting material, and connect with your fans.

• Use paid advertising on networks like Facebook and Instagram for targeted campaigns.

3. Email Marketing:

• Build an email list of interested prospects and customers.

• Send tailored and useful information, promotions, and updates to your subscribers.

• Segment your email list for more focused promotions.

4. Content Marketing:

• Create a content plan that includes blog entries, articles, videos, and infographics.

• Share your skills and bring answers to your audience's challenges.

• Promote your material via social media and email.

5. Pay-Per-Click (PPC) Advertising:

• Use platforms like Google advertising to develop sponsored search and display advertising.

• Target certain keywords to attract prospective clients who are actively looking for your goods or services.

6. Influencer Marketing:

• Collaborate with influencers in your business to reach their fans.

• Choose influencers whose audience corresponds with your target market.

7. Online Events and Webinars:

• Host webinars or online events to educate and engage your audience.

• Use interactive features to build a feeling of community.

8. Online Reviews and Reputation Management:

• Encourage pleased customers to submit good reviews on networks like Google My Business and Yelp.

• Respond to both good and negative feedback professionally and immediately.

Offline Marketing Techniques

1. Print Advertising:

• Create print products such as brochures, flyers, and business cards.

• Distribute these brochures at local events, trade exhibits, and in your neighborhood.

2. Direct Mail:

• Send direct mail campaigns to specific targets.

• Use postcards, letters, or catalogs to market your goods or services.

3. Networking and Relationship Building:

• Attend local business networking events and industry conferences.

• Build ties with other companies and future clients.

4. Community Involvement:

• Participate in community events, fund local activities, or support charity organizations.

• Show your dedication to the local community and interact with future consumers.

5. Trade Shows and Exhibitions:

• Exhibit in trade exhibitions and industry-specific events to display your goods and services.

• Engage with attendees and create leads.

6. Cold Calling and Direct Sales:

• Reach out to prospective customers via phone calls or in-person meetings.

• Build a sales staff to participate in direct sales operations.

7. Print Media:

• Place advertising in local newspapers or publications that appeal to your target demographic.

• Include contact information and a compelling call to action.

8. Billboards & Outdoor Advertising:

• Use billboards, bus advertisements, and other outdoor advertising to improve brand exposure.

• Create eye-catching designs and clear messages.

9. Radio and Television Advertising:

• Invest in radio or TV advertising to reach a large audience.

• Craft distinctive and compelling ad content.

Effective marketing generally entails mixing online and offline strategies to attract a wide audience and optimize your brand's visibility. Customize your marketing approach depending on your target market's interests and habits, and frequently review the efficacy of each channel to make informed improvements.

CHAPTER 12

SALES AND CUSTOMER ACQUISITION

Sales Strategies and Techniques

Effective sales methods and approaches are vital for developing your client base and earning income. Whether you're selling items or services, recognizing the main principles of effective sales is vital. Here are some methods and approaches to help you reach your sales goals:

1. Build Strong Customer Relationships

Building and sustaining great client connections is the basis of effective sales. Focus on:

• Active Listening: Listen to your clients' wants and problems to deliver solutions that suit their criteria.

• Personalization: Tailor your approach to each consumer, indicating that you understand their wants and preferences.

• Follow-up: After a transaction, continue to connect with consumers, giving help and guaranteeing their pleasure.

2. Value-Based Selling

Shift your emphasis from selling things or services to selling value. Show them how your goods can solve their issues or satisfy their wants. Emphasize:

• Benefits Over Features: Highlight the benefits and advantages of your services rather than merely listing features.

• Solutions-Oriented Approach: Present your goods or services as solutions to particular issues or difficulties your clients face.

3. Sales Funnel Management

Understand and manage your sales funnel to move clients from early awareness to completing a purchase. The phases often include:

• Awareness: Create brand awareness via marketing and advertising.

• attention: Capture the attention of prospective consumers with interesting content and offers.

• Consideration: Provide extensive information and handle client inquiries to support decision-making.

• Purchase: Close the deal with a clear call to action.

4. Effective Communication

Effective communication is at the core of effective sales. Develop your communication abilities by:

• Clear Messaging: Communicate your value offer simply and succinctly.

• Building Rapport: Establish a relationship with consumers by being warm, personable, and empathic.

• Objection Handling: Be prepared to handle objections or concerns with confidence and solutions.

5. Upselling and Cross-Selling

Increase revenue by providing clients with additional or enhanced items or services. This may enhance the average transaction value. Key tactics include:

• Product Bundles: Offer packaged bundles that bring extra value.

• Recommendations: Suggest complementary items or services that improve the customer's purchase.

6. Sales Process Optimization

Optimize your sales process for efficiency and effectiveness. Consider:

• Sales Scripts: Develop scripts or templates to maintain uniformity in your sales team's approach.

• Sales Training: Provide continual training to your sales force to maintain their skills up to date.

• Sales Tools: Equip your staff with the necessary tools, such as CRM software, to expedite operations.

7. Follow-Up and After-Sales Service

Your connection with clients doesn't stop with a transaction. Maintain the connection by:

• Follow-up calls and Emails: Check in with clients to verify they're happy and fix any concerns.

• input Collection: Seek input to enhance your goods or services.

• Loyalty Programs: Offer loyalty prizes to promote repeat business.

8. Data-Driven Sales

Use data and analytics to inform your sales efforts. This includes:

• consumer Segmentation: Segment your consumer base to customize your approach to various groups.

• Sales Performance indicators: Track critical indicators including conversion rates, average order value, and client acquisition cost.

• A/B Testing: Experiment with various sales methods to determine the most successful strategies.

9. Sales Team Collaboration

If you have a sales staff, promote teamwork and information exchange. Team members may learn from one another and assist one another in achieving.

10. Continuous Improvement

Continuously review and improve your sales methods. Regularly analyze your performance, receive input from your staff and consumers, and make appropriate modifications.

Effective sales methods and approaches vary throughout time as consumer tastes and markets change. By keeping customer-centric and focused on creating connections, giving value, and adjusting to market developments, you can boost your sales efforts and generate company success.

Building a Customer Base

A strong firm relies on a solid and developing client base. Here are tactics and approaches to help you establish and expand your client base effectively:

1. Understand Your Ideal Customer

Begin by identifying your ideal client. Create thorough customer personas that incorporate demographics, habits, needs, and pain areas. This information will influence your marketing and sales activities.

2. Market Research

Conduct rigorous market research to discover possible client categories. Analyze industry trends, competitive tactics, and consumer preferences to customize your offers and marketing techniques.

3. Lead Generation

Generate leads via different means, including:

• material Marketing: Create quality material that draws prospective clients to your website or social media channels.

• Email Marketing: Build your email list and provide relevant content and offers to nurture leads.

• Social Media: Utilize social media channels to communicate with prospective clients and boost traffic to your website.

• Search Engine Optimization (SEO): Optimize your web content to rank better in search results, boosting organic traffic.

4. Content Marketing

Produce high-quality content that educates, entertains, or solves problems for your target audience. Share this material via blog articles, videos, infographics, and social media.

5. Inbound Marketing

Implement inbound marketing strategies that attract potential customers to your business by providing them with valuable and relevant content. This can include blogs, eBooks, and webinars.

6. Referral Marketing

Encourage existing customers to refer new ones by offering incentives or rewards for successful referrals.

7. Networking and Partnerships

Build relationships with other businesses or individuals that cater to your target audience. Collaborate on events, promotions, or content to access each other's customer bases.

8. Advertising

Use online and offline advertising to reach a broader audience. Online advertising options include pay-per-click (PPC), social media ads, and display ads. Offline options include print ads and billboards.

9. Website Optimization

Ensure your website is optimized for lead generation and customer acquisition:

• Clear Calls to Action (CTAs): Include appealing CTAs that encourage visitors to take action, such as signing up for a newsletter or completing a purchase.

• Landing Pages: Create dedicated landing pages for specific offers, ensuring a clear path for conversion.

• User Experience (UX): Make your website user-friendly and responsive, offering a seamless experience on all devices.

10. Email Marketing

Leverage email marketing to nurture leads and convert them into customers. Create tailored email campaigns and automation to guide leads through the sales funnel.

11. Sales Funnels

Design sales funnels that guide potential customers through a series of steps, from awareness to consideration to purchase.

12. Customer Retention

Keep existing customers engaged and satisfied. A satisfied customer is more likely to become a loyal customer and recommend your business to others.

13. Customer Relationship Management (CRM) Tools

Utilize CRM software to manage customer relationships, gather data, and streamline communications. This can help you personalize interactions and improve customer service.

14. Surveys and Feedback

Gather feedback from customers and leads to better understand their needs and preferences. Use this information to tailor your offerings and marketing.

15. Loyalty Programs

Implement loyalty programs to reward repeat customers. Encourage them to keep coming back and referring others.

16. Analyze and Optimize

Regularly analyze data to assess the effectiveness of your customer acquisition strategies. Use key performance indicators (KPIs) to measure your success and make data-driven optimizations.

17. Continuous Learning

Stay updated with industry trends and customer behavior. The more you know about your target audience, the better you can tailor your strategies for customer acquisition.

Building a customer base is an ongoing process that requires a deep understanding of your target audience and a multifaceted approach. By employing a combination of these strategies and techniques, you can steadily grow your customer base and foster long-term relationships with satisfied clients.

13

OPERATIONS AND PROCESSES

Streamlining Business Operations

Streamlining your company processes is the key to boosting productivity, decreasing expenses, and eventually reaching increased profitability. Here are tactics and approaches to assist you in improving your operations:

1. Process Mapping

Start by mapping out your current procedures. Create clear graphic representations of how labor flows inside your business. Identify bottlenecks, redundancies, and places that might be streamlined.

2. Identify Inefficiencies

Identify inefficiencies in your operations, such as:

• Manual operations: Automate repeated manual operations to save time and decrease mistakes.

• Overlapping Roles: Ensure that roles and duties are clearly defined, preventing duplication of effort.

• outmoded Technology: Update outmoded systems and software to boost efficiency.

3. Automation

Implement automation whenever possible. Use software and technologies to automate operations like as data input, order processing, and inventory management. This lowers human mistakes and frees up personnel for more productive tasks.

4. Standard Operating Procedures (SOPs)

Develop explicit SOPs for critical procedures. SOPs offer consistent, step-by-step guidance for staff, ensuring that activities are done accurately and effectively.

5. Employee Training

Invest in staff training to guarantee that your team is well-equipped to manage their duties effectively. Well-trained staff are more likely to simplify procedures and boost efficiency.

6. Inventory Management

Optimize your inventory management to cut carrying costs and avoid overstock or stockouts. Use forecasting strategies to ensure you have the proper quantity of inventory on hand.

7. Supply Chain Management

Evaluate your supply chain and discover opportunities for improvement. Streamlining your supply chain may cut lead times, save costs, and boost dependability.

8. Outsourcing

Consider outsourcing non-core operations, like as customer assistance, accounting, or IT services, to specialist service providers. This might free up your internal resources for more strategic duties.

9. Vendor Relationships

Cultivate good ties with your suppliers. Negotiate advantageous conditions, investigate volume savings, and seek collaborations that might boost your supply chain efficiency.

10. Performance Metrics

Establish key performance indicators (KPIs) to measure the efficiency of your activities. Regularly monitor and evaluate these indicators to find areas that need improvement.

11. Quality Control

Implement comprehensive quality control techniques to verify that goods or services satisfy your requirements. Reducing faults and rework may save both time and money.

12. Lean Principles

Adopt lean concepts to decrease waste and improve processes. Focus on removing non-value-added activities, lowering lead times, and enhancing overall productivity.

13. Technology Integration

Integrate your technological systems and tools for smooth data exchange and collaboration. A unified IT infrastructure helps simplify operations across departments.

14. Cross-Training

Cross-train your personnel so they can manage different responsibilities as required. This flexibility may boost efficiency during busy times or workforce shortages.

15. Continuous Improvement

Promote a culture of constant improvement. Encourage staff to spot inefficiencies and recommend fixes. Regularly examine and modify your procedures.

16. Cost Management

Examine your expenditures carefully and seek methods to cut overhead. This may entail renegotiating contracts, decreasing energy use, or optimizing office space utilization.

Streamlining your company processes is a continual endeavor. Regularly examine your procedures, receive input from your staff, and keep open to technology improvements that might further increase efficiency. By consistently researching methods to improve your processes, you may develop a more competitive and lucrative firm.

Inventory Management and Supply Chain Optimization

Efficient inventory management and a well-optimized supply chain are crucial for minimizing costs and guaranteeing a seamless flow of goods and services. Here are ways and approaches to increase your inventory management and supply chain:

Inventory Management:

1. Demand Forecasting: Use past data and market patterns to estimate future demand. This helps you order the proper quantity of products and minimize stockouts or overstocking.

2. Just-in-Time (JIT) Inventory: Implement a JIT system to receive inventory when required, lowering storage costs and the danger of outdated inventory.

3. ABC Analysis: Categorize inventory items into A, B, and C categories depending on their significance. Focus on strictly controlling A thing while retaining less rigorous control over C goods.

4. Safety Stock: Maintain a buffer of safety stock to accommodate for unanticipated demand changes or supply chain interruptions.

5. FIFO and LIFO: Use the First-In, First-Out (FIFO) or Last-In, First-Out (LIFO) approach to control the order in which items are

sold, depending on your company requirements and inventory characteristics.

6. Supplier ties: Build good ties with suppliers to negotiate better terms, gain discounts, and assure timely delivery.

7. Inventory Turnover: Calculate and monitor inventory turnover ratios. Higher turnover shows that your merchandise is moving efficiently.

8. Technology Solutions: Invest in inventory management software to automate activities, monitor stock levels, and provide reports for improved decision-making.

Supply Chain Optimization:

9. source Diversification: Avoid depending on a single source for crucial components. Diversify your supply base to lessen the chance of interruptions.

10. Lead Time Reduction: Work with suppliers to minimize lead times. Faster lead times enable you to adapt to shifting demand more effectively.

11. Transportation Efficiency: Optimize transportation routes and carriers to decrease shipping costs and delivery times.

12. Warehousing and Distribution: Efficiently manage your warehouse, ensuring that things are housed logically and simple to retrieve.

13. Reverse Logistics: Streamline the return process for items, decreasing the cost and hassle of handling returns and exchanges.

14. Quality Control: Implement stringent quality control methods to minimize faulty items and decrease rework.

15. Sustainability: Consider sustainable and ecologically responsible supply chain techniques to fulfill growing customer demands and decrease environmental impact.

16. Collaborative Planning: Collaborate closely with suppliers and distributors to synchronize production timelines, quantities, and other logistical issues.

17. Risk Management: Develop a risk management plan to handle unexpected disruptions, such as natural disasters or geopolitical events, which might damage the supply chain.

18. Supply Chain Technology: Leverage supply chain management software and technology, such as IoT (Internet of Things) sensors, to obtain real-time insight into your supply chain.

19. Continuous Evaluation: Continuously examine and evaluate the performance of your supply chain partners, making improvements as required.

20. Cost Analysis: Regularly assess the cost structure of your supply chain to discover areas where you may decrease expenditures without sacrificing quality or efficiency.

Effective inventory management and supply chain efficiency demand a proactive approach. By continually evaluating and improving these parts of your operations, you may generate cost savings and provide goods and services more effectively to fulfill client demand.

14

TEAM BUILDING AND MANAGEMENT

Hiring, Training, and Managing Employees

A talented and motivated crew is the backbone of a successful firm. Here's how you create, train, and manage a high-performing workforce:

Hiring:

1. Describe job tasks: Clearly describe the tasks and responsibilities for each job. Create thorough job descriptions to attract the appropriate people.

2. Recruitment plan: Develop a recruitment plan that includes job posts, referrals, and partnerships with recruiting firms or platforms.

3. Cultural Fit: Assess applicants not just for their abilities and experience but also for their cultural fit with your business.

4. Structured Interviews: Conduct structured interviews using a series of preset questions to guarantee a fair assessment of prospects.

5. Skills Assessment: Use skills exams or assessments to determine applicants' proficiency in relevant areas.

6. Reference Checks: Check references to check applicants' employment history and credentials.

7. Onboarding: Create an organized onboarding process to acquaint new personnel with business policy, culture, and work expectations.

Training:

8. Employee Development Plan: Develop tailored employee development plans that match their career aspirations and the company's requirements.

9. abilities Training: Provide training programs to develop workers' abilities, whether they be technical, interpersonal, or leadership skills.

10. mentoring Programs: Implement mentoring programs that link experienced personnel with newbies for assistance and information exchange.

11. Regular comments: Conduct regular performance evaluations and give constructive comments to assist staff development.

12. continual Learning: Encourage continual learning and self-improvement via workshops, seminars, and online courses.

13. Cross-Training: Cross-train people to execute numerous tasks, boosting team flexibility and information exchange.

Managing:

14. Leadership Development: Invest in leadership development to grow future managers from within your team.

15. Clear Communication: Maintain open and transparent communication with your team. Share corporate objectives, updates, and expectations often.

16. Team Meetings: Conduct frequent team meetings to review accomplishments, issues, and objectives. Encourage team members to provide ideas and comments.

17. Performance Metrics: Establish explicit performance metrics and key performance indicators (KPIs) for each position. Monitor and assess performance against these measures.

18. Recognition & Rewards: Recognize and recognize workers for their efforts. This may be via bonuses, promotions, or non-monetary benefits like employee of the month honors.

19. Conflict Resolution: Address workplace issues swiftly and professionally, giving mediation or help where required.

20. Wellness Programs: Promote employee well-being via wellness programs that include physical and mental health assistance.

21. Flexible Work Arrangements: Consider giving flexible work arrangements to fit varied employee demands, such as remote work choices or flexible scheduling.

22. Succession Planning: Develop a succession plan to identify and train future leaders to fill important roles when they become available.

23. Empowerment: Empower your team by allowing them the liberty to make choices within their jobs, establishing a feeling of ownership.

24. Regular Performance assessments: Conduct yearly or semi-annual performance assessments to establish objectives, evaluate performance, and discuss career advancement.

25. Exit Interviews: Conduct exit interviews with leaving workers to get insights about areas for growth within your firm.

Effective team development and management include a commitment to investing in your team's growth and well-being. By recruiting the appropriate people, offering training and development, and practicing good management, you can establish a motivated and talented staff that contributes to the success of your organization.

Building a Strong Company Culture

A good corporate culture generates a pleasant work environment, encourages employee happiness, and supports business success. Here's how you establish and foster a good corporate culture:

1. Define Core Values:

• Clearly explain the essential principles that your organization stands for. These values should govern decision-making, conduct, and relationships inside the company.

2. Lead by Example:

• Leadership sets the tone for the organizational culture. Leaders should embrace the key principles and display the actions they demand from staff.

3. Employee Involvement:

• Involve workers in developing the corporate culture. Encourage their involvement in developing values, purpose, and objectives.

4. Clear Mission and Vision:

• Develop a clear and appealing mission and vision statement that articulates the company's purpose and long-term objectives.

5. Communication:

• Foster open and transparent communication at all levels of the company. Encourage frequent feedback and conversation.

6. Empowerment:

• Empower workers by offering them autonomy and decision-making ability inside their jobs. This instills a feeling of ownership.

7. Diversity and Inclusion:

• Promote diversity and inclusion inside your workplace. Create an inclusive workplace where various viewpoints are appreciated.

8. Recognition & Appreciation:

• Recognize and recognize workers' efforts. Celebrate successes and milestones.

9. Employee Development:

• Invest in staff development and growth. Provide possibilities for study, training, and job progression.

10. Work-Life Balance:

• Encourage work-life balance and flexibility to promote workers' well-being.

11. Wellness Programs:

• Implement wellness programs that encourage physical and mental health, including exercise efforts and stress management resources.

12. Team Building Activities:

• Organize team-building activities and events to enhance connections among staff.

13. Values-Based Decision-Making:

• Make values-based decision-making a part of your company's culture. Ensure that choices match your fundamental beliefs and objectives.

14. Feedback Mechanisms:

• Establish feedback channels that enable workers to express their issues, give comments, and provide solutions.

15. Company Traditions:

• Create and preserve organizational traditions and rituals that support the culture, such as yearly celebrations, awards, or team-building activities.

16. Continuous Improvement:

• Regularly analyze and enhance your corporate culture. Be receptive to improvements that enhance the working atmosphere.

17. Sustainability and Corporate Responsibility:

• Integrate sustainability and corporate social responsibility activities into your business culture. This might indicate a dedication to ethical behaviors.

18. Conflict Resolution:

• Develop a systematic strategy for conflict resolution that ensures conflicts are handled professionally and equitably.

19. Mentorship Programs:

• Establish mentoring programs to promote the growth and development of workers, particularly those in the early phases of their careers.

20. Community Engagement:

• Engage with the community and support charity projects, integrating your company's culture with a sense of social responsibility.

A good business culture is not something that emerges quickly; it's a continual endeavor that demands attention and consistency. By focusing on core values, communication, employee well-being, and continual development, you can establish and sustain a strong business culture that recruits, keeps, and encourages your team.

15

SCALING YOUR BUSINESS

Expanding Your Business

Expanding your company is an exciting yet demanding venture. Here are tactics and approaches to assist you in effectively expand your business:

1. Market Research:

• Conduct thorough market research to find chances for development. Analyze consumer demand, competition, and market trends.

2. Growth plan:

• Develop a clear growth plan that defines your expansion objectives, target markets, and timescales.

3. company Plan:

• Update your company plan to match with your growth strategy. Include financial predictions, marketing initiatives, and operational adjustments.

4. finance:

• Secure the required finance to sustain growth, whether via savings, loans, investors, or crowdsourcing.

5. Expand Product/Service Offerings:

• Consider expanding your product or service offerings to attract a larger consumer base or cater to new markets.

6. Geographic Expansion:

• Explore chances to grow into new geographic regions, either locally or worldwide.

7. Online Presence:

• Enhance your online presence to reach a bigger audience. This may include developing e-commerce platforms or employing digital marketing to target certain geographies.

8. Partnerships and Alliances:

• Form strategic partnerships or alliances with other firms to leverage their client base and resources.

9. Franchising:

• Consider franchising your company concept to duplicate your success in multiple regions with local operators.

10. personnel and Talent:

• Assess your personnel requirements and acquire additional talent as appropriate. Focus on recruiting people who match your company's beliefs and ambitions.

11. Systems and procedures:

• Streamline and automate internal procedures to meet rising demand and operational complexity.

12. Marketing and Advertising:

• Invest in marketing and advertising techniques that target your expanding markets. Tailor your messaging to local tastes if growing globally.

13. Customer Support:

• Enhance customer support and service skills to retain client satisfaction as your firm expands.

14. Supply Chain and Logistics:

• Optimize your supply chain and logistics to suit rising production and distribution needs.

15. Risk Management:

• Evaluate possible risks connected with growth and establish a risk management plan to reduce them.

16. Legal and Regulatory Compliance:

• Ensure your firm complies with all necessary legal and regulatory standards in new markets.

17. Customer input:

• Collect and evaluate customer input to react to changing market demands and enhance your goods or services.

18. Monitor Key Metrics:

• Continuously monitor key performance indicators (KPIs) to measure the effectiveness of your growth activities.

19. Scaling Culture:

• Maintain your business culture as you develop, ensuring that it corresponds with your fundamental values and creates a healthy work environment.

20. Exit plan:

- Consider an exit plan for your firm, whether via a merger, acquisition, or public offering, to maximize on your success.

Expanding your firm is a huge step, and it demands comprehensive strategy and execution. Be flexible, adaptive, and ready to learn from the obstacles and triumphs of the growth process. By carefully evaluating these methods and approaches, you may negotiate the challenges of development and accomplish your expansion objectives.

Franchising and Partnerships

Franchising and developing strategic alliances are important ways to increase your firm. Here's how to properly use these development avenues:

Franchising:

1. Franchise Model Evaluation: Assess if your firm is suited for franchising. A good franchise model often features a well-defined and reproducible idea.

2. Legal and Regulatory Compliance: Familiarize yourself with franchise legislation in your location and verify that your franchise disclosure papers conform with legal standards.

3. Franchise Business Plan: Develop a detailed franchise business plan that includes the franchise structure, fees, and assistance you'll give to franchisees.

4. Franchisee Selection: Be careful in picking franchisees who share your company's principles and can repeat your success.

5. Training and assistance: Establish a thorough training program and continuing assistance for franchisees to ensure they understand and apply your business model efficiently.

6. Operations Handbook: Create a complete operations handbook that aids franchisees in managing day-to-day activities and preserving your brand standards.

7. Marketing and Branding: Develop a marketing plan to promote the franchise opportunity and maintain consistent branding across all locations.

8. Quality Control: Implement quality control methods to guarantee that franchisees retain the same product or service standards.

9. Franchisee Relationships: Maintain open and friendly relationships with franchisees to enhance cooperation and mutual success.

10. Performance Metrics: Monitor the performance of franchise sites using key performance indicators (KPIs) and give comments and improvement ideas.

Partnerships:

11. Strategic Alignment: Seek alliances that connect with your company's aims and beliefs. Identify partners that have a comparable client base or complementary goods and services.

12. explicit aims: Establish explicit aims and goals for the collaboration, including what each member intends to accomplish.

13. Legal Agreements: Draft legal agreements that explain the conditions and duties of each partner. It's necessary to preserve both sides' interests.

14. Collaborative Marketing: Collaborate on marketing projects that promote both businesses, using each other's consumer base and resources.

15. Shared Resources: Share resources and knowledge to increase the quality and efficiency of goods or services.

16. Mutual Benefits: Ensure that the collaboration is mutually beneficial, giving benefits to both parties involved.

17. contact: Maintain frequent and open contact with your partners to handle difficulties and opportunities swiftly.

18. assess outcomes: Continuously assess the outcomes of the collaboration and analyze its influence on your company goals.

19. adjust and develop: Be ready to adjust and develop the collaboration as circumstances change or as new possibilities emerge.

20. Exit plan: Consider an exit plan for the collaboration in case it no longer matches your company's aims.

Franchising and developing strategic alliances may greatly extend your company's reach and income possibilities. However, it's vital to approach these techniques with careful preparation, detailed legal considerations, and a dedication to creating great relationships with franchisees and partners. Successful franchises and partnerships may be a crucial driver of corporate development.

16

MANAGING FINANCES FOR GROWTH

Financial Planning for Long-Term Success

Effective financial planning is the cornerstone of long-term company success and development. Here are some ideas and approaches to handle your funds strategically:

1. Financial Forecasting:

• Develop complete financial forecasts, including income statements, balance sheets, and cash flow statements, to estimate revenue, costs, and cash flow.

2. Budgeting:

• Create a precise budget that details your estimated income and spending for the forthcoming term. Continuously compare actual performance to the budget.

3. funds Allocation:

• Carefully distribute funds to diverse elements of your firm, including operations, marketing, growth, and debt reduction.

4. Working Capital Management:

• Manage working capital effectively by managing accounts receivable, accounts payable, and inventory levels.

5. Debt Management:

• Assess your debt structure and design a plan for managing and lowering debt while minimizing interest payments.

6. Investment Decisions:

• Evaluate possible investments, such as new equipment, technology, or expansions, to estimate their potential return on investment (ROI).

7. Emergency reserve:

• Maintain an emergency reserve to meet unforeseen costs or economic downturns.

8. Profit Margins:

• Monitor and increase profit margins via cost reduction, pricing strategies, and value-added services.

9. Cash Flow Management:

• Implement initiatives to increase cash flow, including negotiating better payment terms with suppliers and speeding receivables collection.

10. Financial Ratios:

• Regularly assess financial ratios including liquidity, profitability, and solvency to acquire insights into your business's financial health.

11. Risk Management:

• Identify financial risks and establish measures to manage them, such as insurance coverage for unanticipated occurrences.

12. Tax Planning:

• Engage in smart tax planning to decrease your tax burden lawfully, optimizing your available resources.

13. Investment Diversification:

• Diversify your assets to lessen risk. Consider investing outside your primary business.

14. Contingency Planning:

• Develop contingency plans for different financial circumstances, letting you respond to unforeseen developments successfully.

15. Long-Term Financial objectives:

• Set clear long-term financial objectives for your organization, which might include obtaining a set amount of sales, profitability, or market share.

16. Reinvestment:

• Reinvest earnings into the firm for growth and development rather than dispersing them to stakeholders.

17. examine and Adjustment:

• Continuously examine your financial plans and alter them in response to changing market circumstances, company performance, and economic trends.

18. Professional Financial Advice:

• Consider receiving counsel from financial experts or accountants to help you make educated financial choices.

19. Financial Education:

• Invest in financial education for yourself and key team members to ensure everyone understands and participates in the financial planning process.

20. Exit Strategy:

• Develop an exit strategy that explains your intentions for departing or transitioning the firm, which might include selling, transferring it to family, or going public.

Strategic financial planning is a continuous activity that changes with your organization. By constantly managing your money, creating clear long-term objectives, and making educated choices, you can safeguard your business's financial health and assure long-term success and development.

Avoiding Common Financial Pitfalls

To achieve financial success and support long-term development, it's vital to be aware of and avoid frequent financial hazards that might jeopardize your organization. Here are some tips for avoiding clear of financial challenges:

1. Overspending:

• Maintain rigorous budget management and minimize superfluous expenses. Regularly examine and change your budget to ensure it corresponds with your financial objectives.

2. Inadequate Cash Reserves:

• Always keep a sufficient cash reserve to meet unforeseen expenditures and to guarantee you can continue operating during lean times.

3. Excessive Debt:

• Be careful while taking on debt. Keep a sustainable debt-to-equity ratio and ensure that loans are utilized for investments that produce returns.

4. Poor Credit Management:

• Maintain a solid credit score and monitor your company credit to achieve advantageous terms and financing possibilities.

5. Neglecting Risk Management:

• Identify and handle possible financial risks, such as market swings, legal concerns, and operational obstacles.

6. Inadequate Insurance Coverage:

• Ensure you have proper insurance coverage to guard against unanticipated disasters that might harm your organization.

7. Overreliance on a Single client:

• Diversify your client base to lessen the risk associated with depending too heavily on a single source of income.

8. Ignoring Financial Statements:

• Regularly examine and evaluate your financial statements to acquire insights into your business's performance and find development opportunities.

9. Inefficient Tax Planning:

• Work with tax specialists to improve your tax plan, decreasing your tax burden lawfully.

10. Neglecting Employee Benefits:

• Invest in employee benefits to attract and retain top people, while also enhancing morale and productivity.

11. Inadequate Pricing Strategies:

• Set pricing that represents the value of your goods or services and pay your expenditures. Avoid underpricing, which might lead to financial troubles.

12. Poor Inventory Management:

• Optimize your inventory management to minimize overstock or stockouts, which may tie up money or lead to missed sales.

13. Not Planning for development:

• Anticipate the financial needs of company development, including increased employment, infrastructure, and marketing expenditures.

14. Neglecting Compliance:

• Stay informed with legal and regulatory standards to prevent penalties and fines that might strain your resources.

15. Lack of Financial Education:

• Continuously educate yourself and your team on financial problems to make educated choices and avoid expensive blunders.

16. Failing to Adapt:

• Be nimble and adaptive. Monitor market movements and be ready to alter your financial plan to suit changing conditions.

17. Ignoring Customer input:

• Listen to customer input and utilize it to better your goods, services, and overall customer experience.

18. No Exit plan:

• Develop an exit plan to give a clear route ahead in case you need to depart the firm or pass it over to others.

By avoiding these typical financial traps and proactively resolving financial issues, you can secure the financial health and stability of your organization, setting the way for sustainable development and long-term success.

17

TROUBLESHOOTING AND CHALLENGES

Dealing with Setbacks and Failures

Setbacks and setbacks are an inherent part of the business path. How you react to these obstacles may dramatically affect your business's future success. Here are tactics and approaches for efficiently coping with setbacks and failures:

1. Resilience:

• Cultivate resilience by building the capacity to bounce back from hardship. Understand that failures are a normal part of business and utilize them as chances for progress.

2. Learn from Mistakes:

• View failures as great learning experiences. Analyze what went wrong and discover solutions to prevent making the same errors.

3. Adaptability:

• Be open to change and adjust to unanticipated situations. A flexible company approach helps you to pivot and identify new solutions.

4. Positive Mindset:

• Maintain a positive attitude and concentrate on solutions rather than concentrating on difficulties. A positive mentality may promote creativity and problem-solving.

5. Seek insight:

• Reach out to mentors, business advisers, or industry colleagues for insight and support when confronting severe obstacles. Their experience may bring useful insights.

6. Stress Management:

• Implement stress management practices to preserve your well-being throughout stressful times. Exercise, meditation, and time management may help reduce stress.

7. Contingency Planning:

• Develop contingency plans to prepare for any obstacles. Having a strategy in place may help you react efficiently in times of crisis.

8. Financial Reserves:

• Maintain financial reserves to buffer your firm during downturns or unforeseen costs.

9. Customer input:

• Listen to customer input and utilize it as a guide for enhancing your goods and services. Customers' viewpoints might identify problems that require addressing.

10. Team Support:

• Involve and inspire your team to solve obstacles together. Encourage open communication and cooperation.

11. Decision-Making:

• Make educated and reasoned judgments based on evidence and analysis rather than responding emotionally to setbacks.

12. Evaluate Risk Tolerance:

• Regularly analyze your risk tolerance and change your strategy appropriately. Consider if some risks are worth incurring.

13. ongoing Improvement:

• Embrace a culture of ongoing improvement, where failures become opportunities to refine procedures and boost efficiency.

14. Network Building:

• Cultivate a network of peers and connections who can give advice and support during hard times.

15. strategy Planning:

• Reevaluate your long-term strategy plan in light of failures, revising your aims and objectives as appropriate.

16. Persistence:

• Keep going ahead, especially when confronted with hurdles. Persistence is frequently the key to overcoming hardship.

17. appreciate triumphs:

• Don't forget to appreciate your triumphs, even tiny ones. Recognizing successes may enhance morale and motivation.

18. Seek Inspiration:

• Read success stories, profiles of great entrepreneurs, and motivational books to get inspiration during trying times.

19. Acceptance:

• Accept that not every problem can be conquered, and there may be occasions when the wisest solution is to cut your losses and move on to other chances.

20. Balance:

• preserve a balance between your personal and work life to avoid burnout and preserve mental and emotional well-being.

Dealing with setbacks and failures is a vital aspect of the entrepreneurial path. By adopting these methods and approaches, you may not only overcome problems but also utilize them as stepping stones toward future achievement.

Overcoming Obstacles

Obstacles are a normal part of the business path. Overcoming them needs resilience, ingenuity, and a deliberate approach. Here are essential ways for successfully overcoming obstacles:

1. Problem Solving:

• Develop a methodical problem-solving technique that helps you to break down complicated difficulties into smaller, manageable components.

2. Analyze fundamental Causes:

• Identify the fundamental causes of difficulties rather than only addressing surface-level concerns. This enables more effective and durable solutions.

3. Seek competence:

• When confronted with difficulties beyond your competence, consult with experts, mentors, or advisers who can give insight and solutions.

4. Adaptability:

• Be flexible and open to change. The capacity to adjust to changing situations is vital for overcoming unanticipated hurdles.

5. Continuous Learning:

• Embrace a culture of continuous learning inside your organization, where staff are encouraged to seek knowledge and adapt to new information.

6. Resilience:

• Cultivate resilience by developing the capacity to bounce back from setbacks and retain a positive outlook.

7. Collaboration:

• Collaborate with your team and harness their combined experience and creativity to solve difficulties.

8. Risk Management:

• Develop a risk management plan that predicts possible hurdles and explains techniques for minimizing them.

9. Stress Management:

• Implement stress management practices to preserve your well-being and decision-making skills during hard situations.

10. Facts-Driven choices:

• Base choices on facts and analysis rather than depending entirely on intuition or gut reactions.

11. Prioritize:

• Prioritize the most significant concerns and handle them first, rather than trying to tackle every hurdle simultaneously.

12. Persistence:

• Persevere through barriers, even when progress is sluggish or setbacks occur. Consistent work typically leads to success.

13. Feedback Loop:

• Create a feedback loop that enables workers and consumers to share their views and suggestions for improvement.

14. review outcomes:

• Continually review the outcomes of your efforts to overcome hurdles and alter your techniques as appropriate.

15. Long-Term Focus:

• Maintain a long-term perspective, realizing that overcoming barriers may need time and patience.

16. Risk Tolerance:

• Assess your risk tolerance and make educated judgments about which challenges are worth overcoming and which are best avoided.

17. Contingency Plans:

• Develop contingency plans to prepare for unforeseen hurdles and catastrophes. Being prepared may help you react more successfully.

18. Adapt and Evolve:

• Be open to revising your company model, strategy, or goods in response to changing market circumstances or unanticipated challenges.

19. Stay updated:

• Stay updated about industry trends, new technology, and prospective disruptors that might pose difficulties or generate opportunities.

20. Seek Inspiration:

• Seek inspiration from successful entrepreneurs, corporate leaders, or historical people who have surmounted tremendous hurdles.

Obstacles might be difficult, but they also provide possibilities for development and advancement. By handling issues with these tactics and having a positive, adaptive mentality, you may successfully overcome hurdles and move your organization ahead.

18

EXIT STRATEGIES

Options for Exiting Your Business

When the time comes to quit your firm, it's crucial to have a clear plan in place. Here are the major choices for quitting your firm, including selling, merging, and succession:

1. Selling Your Business:

• Sale to an Individual: You may sell your firm to an individual buyer who is interested in taking over and operating the company. This option may be excellent if you wish to see your firm continue under new ownership.

• Sale to a rival: Selling to a rival may be a strategic decision, as it may allow for consolidation and the ability to gain synergies and cost savings.

• Private Equity or Venture Capital: Consider selling a piece of your company to private equity or venture capital organizations. This may give an influx of funds for expansion and perhaps an eventual exit.

• IPO (Initial Public Offering): Taking your firm public via an IPO enables you to offer shares to the public, giving a major cash inflow and liquidity. It's a difficult procedure that needs compliance with regulatory regulations.

2. Merging Your Business:

• Merger with a rival: A merger with a rival may lead to greater market share and synergistic advantages. Ensure that the combined company is stronger and more competitive.

• Strategic collaboration: Establish a strategic collaboration with another firm that entails sharing resources, customers, or technology. This may lead to an eventual merger or acquisition.

3. Succession Planning:

• Family Succession: Passing the company along to family members may retain your heritage and create a feeling of continuity. It needs meticulous preparation and may entail training and mentoring family members.

• Management Buyout: Allow your management team to acquire the firm, giving them a feeling of ownership and a genuine stake in its success.

• Employee Stock Ownership Plan (ESOP): An ESOP entails selling the firm to its workers via a trust. This may produce a strong feeling of employee ownership and engagement.

4. Liquidation:

• Closing and Liquidating: In circumstances when the firm is no longer sustainable or lucrative, you may elect to shut it down and liquidate its assets to settle debts or refund cash to shareholders.

5. Franchising:

• Franchising the firm: If your firm has a successful and reproducible concept, you may franchise it, enabling others to manage their locations while paying you franchise fees and royalties.

6. Licensing:

• Licensing Intellectual Property: If your firm holds significant intellectual property, you may license it to other businesses, collecting royalties in exchange.

7. Partial Sale:

• Partial Sale of Assets or Stock: You may sell a piece of your firm assets or stock to investors or partners, enabling you to keep a degree of engagement or control.

8. Charity or Nonprofit Transition:

• Transition to a Nonprofit: In certain situations, you may consider transferring your firm into a nonprofit or charity organization, especially if it matches your charitable ideals.

Selecting the best exit plan relies on your business's conditions, your aspirations, and your financial demands. Planning properly in advance and getting the assistance of financial and legal specialists is key to a successful exit plan. Remember that the leaving process may take time, so start preparing early to guarantee a seamless transfer.

CONCLUSION

In conclusion, commencing the adventure of establishing a company is both an exciting and tough task. Throughout this book, we have explored the key aspects of entrepreneurship, from defining the entrepreneurial journey and assessing your readiness to finding the right business idea, planning for success, navigating legal and financial considerations, setting up your business, and focusing on marketing, sales, operations, management, and growth.

We have also dug into the necessity of financial planning for long-term success and covered ways to avoid common financial mistakes. Additionally, we have examined the important abilities necessary to cope with failures, overcome barriers, and finally attain your objectives.

Finally, we addressed several exit plans, including selling your firm, combining with others, succession planning, and other alternatives to move from your business when the time is appropriate.

The route of entrepreneurship involves effort, ongoing learning, and adaptation. While the journey may be plagued with problems and failures, it's also rich with chances for personal and professional progress. Your entrepreneurial path is uniquely yours, and it's an experience packed with lessons, successes, and the potential to make a lasting influence.

As you go on with your entrepreneurial pursuits, always remember that success is not only determined by your business's financial prosperity but also by the great influence it may have on your life and the lives of others. By utilizing the ideas and tactics provided in this book, you can navigate the convoluted world of entrepreneurship with more confidence and start yourself on the road to developing a flourishing and gratifying company.

Thank you for taking the time to examine our guide on establishing a company, and we wish you the very best in your entrepreneurial adventure.